THE MICROWAVE COOK BOOK

OF

ANGLO-INDIAN RECIPES

Easy Recipes to cook Anglo-Indian Grub
in a Microwave Oven

Bridget White

THE MICROWAVE COOK BOOK

OF

ANGLO-INDIAN RECIPES

Easy Recipes to cook Anglo-Indian Grub
in a Microwave Oven

Bridget White

The Microwave Cook Book of Anglo-Indian Recipes

First Edition: 2021

CONTENTS

4. BREAKFAST IN A JIFFY

5. MICROWAVE SOUP RECIPES

6. MICROWAVE MULLIGATAWNY SOUPS

16. MICROWAVE FESTIVE SWEETS AND TREATS

17. SOME BASIC CURRY POWDERS

18. ABOUT THE AUTHOR – BRIDGET WHITE ...179

FOREWORD

My name is Bridget White-Kumar. I am a Cookery Book Author and Independent Food Consultant in Colonial Anglo-Indian Cuisine at Bangalore, India.

I have authored 8 Cookery Books on Anglo-Indian Cuisine. My area of expertise is in Colonial Anglo-Indian Food and I have gone through a lot of effort in reviving the old forgotten dishes of the Colonial British Raj Era. My Recipe books are a means of preserving for posterity, the very authentic tastes and flavours of Colonial 'Anglo' India, besides recording for future generations, the unique heritage of the pioneers of Anglo-Indian Cuisine.

One of my Cookery Books, *ANGLO-INDIAN CUISINE – A LEGACY OF FLAVOURS FROM THE PAST* was selected as 'Winner from India' under the Category: *'BEST CULINARY HISTORY BOOK' (COUNTRIES) by GOURMAND INTERNATIONAL SPAIN, GOURMAND WORLD COOK BOOKS AWARDS 2012*

All my cookery books have been very well received all over the world and have received excellent reviews on Amazon from people who bought them. They have served as a guide to many who are keen on cooking Anglo-Indian Dishes. Having brought out these 8 Cookery Books exclusively on Anglo-Indian Cuisine, with simple and easy recipes of dishes that needed to be cooked in a traditional way on the stove top,

I decided it was now time to move into this fast-paced world and keep up with the changing times by cooking the same dishes in a modern, fast and easy way in a Microwave Oven. Thereby, making the cooking process simple and easy but at the same retaining the same flavours and tastes which are synonymous to Anglo-Indian Cuisine.

Through trial and error and many experiments, I have arrived at the exact process, procedure and timings to be followed and the right amounts of ingredients etc. to be used while cooking these Anglo-Indian Dishes. The delicious result is this new book 'THE MICROWAVE COOKBOOK OF ANGLO-INDIAN RECIPES' which shows you how to cook our very own Anglo-Indian Grub in a Microwave Oven!

The recipes are simple and easy to follow and only easily available ingredients have been suggested. While the basic recipe can be made use of, chicken, or vegetables can be substituted for meat and vice versa, by following the given timings for a particular type of meat.
So go ahead and start cooking your favourite Anglo-Indian Dish in your microwave oven in just a few minutes.

Bridget White

ABOUT THE BOOK

THE MICROWAVE COOKBOOK OF ANGLO-INDIAN RECIPES, is an interesting collection of easy- to- follow Recipes of popular and well-loved Anglo-Indian dishes.

I have selected the most popular recipes from all my earlier Anglo-Indian Recipe Books and brought them out in this book. All these recipes have been in my family for generations.

The selection offered in the book ranges from Microwave Breakfast Recipes, Soups, Pepper-Water and Mulligatawny, mouth-watering Curries of Chicken, Meat, Pork, Seafood, Eggs, Vegetarian and Rice dishes, Desserts, Festive Sweets, Home-made Curry Powders, etc., that could be made in a jiffy.

Dishes such as Anglo-Indian Pepper Water, Mulligatawny, Country Captain Chicken, Chicken Jalfrazie, Meat Ball Curry (Bad Word Curry) and Coconut Rice, Railway Mutton Curry, Lamb Stew, Beef Pepper Fry, Pork Vindaloo, Pork Devil Fry, Fish Moley, Prawn Vindaloo, Egg Curries, Vegetable Foogaths and Side Dishes, Pilafs / Pilau of Beef, Mutton, Chicken, are sure to bring on nostalgic memories evocative of a by-gone era. A mixture of East and West to anyone who likes Anglo-Indian food. Desserts and Festive Sweets include the classic Bread Pudding, chocolate and almond fudge, Coconut Sweets (Barfi) and many other popular festive treats.

Special mention should be made of the old popular Anglo-Indian Christmas sweet Dodol or Dhol Dhol - a gooey halwa like sweet made from Black Glutinous Rice and Coconut Milk. This dish takes hours to make in the traditional way but can be made in the microwave in a very short time.

I have also included tips on thawing and defrosting raw food items, reheating cooked food, the type of dishes or containers that should be made use of, how to clean the inside of the microwave, besides many other helpful hints and suggestions for cooking in microwave oven

The easy-to-follow recipes make cooking these old, popular, sumptuous dishes, enjoyable and problem-free in your Microwave. I am confident that anyone who follows these recipes will turn out dishes that will truly be a gastronomic delight besides having a rendezvous with History.

Bridget White

PREFACE

The microwave oven is one of the greatest inventions of the 20th century. Now almost 75% of the world's population use a microwave oven in their homes either to heat up pre-cooked food or to cook a meal.

Microwaves are a quick and convenient way to cook food, and have therefore, made life easier and more convenient. However, a microwave oven needs to be used correctly. A uniform temperature of 75 Degrees Centigrade is needed to cook food evenly in a microwave. Microwave ovens can sometimes cook food unevenly and leave "cold spots" where harmful bacteria can survive.

It is important to cook food at the recommended safe temperature to destroy bacteria and other pathogens that could cause foodborne illness.

The Microwaves penetrate the food to a depth of 1 to 1½ inches. It is therefore advisable to cut foods such as meat or poultry into evenly sized pieces if possible, or put larger or thicker items towards the outside edge of the dish.

In thicker pieces of food, the microwave doesn't reach the center, so that area would cook by conduction of heat from the outer areas of the food into the middle.

In a microwave oven, the air in the oven is at room temperature so the temperature of the food surface is cooler than food in a conventional oven where the food is heated by hot air. Therefore, food cooked in a microwave oven doesn't normally become brown and crispy.

To ensure even and uniform cooking, it is advisable to arrange food items evenly in a covered dish and add some liquid such as water.

Cover the food with a microwave-safe lid or microwave plastic wrap. This will trap the steam and promote more even cooking. The moist heat that is created will also help to destroy harmful bacteria and ensure uniform cooking.

Allow enough space between the food and the top of the dish so that plastic wrap does not touch the food. Loosen or vent the lid or wrap to allow steam to vent.

While cooking meats, it is preferable to make use of boneless meat as bones could hinder the meat from cooking through. Stir, rotate, or turn foods over (where possible) midway through the microwave cooking time to even the cooking and eliminate cold spots.

Wait until the standing time is over before you check that the cooking is complete. Food continues to cook even after the microwave is turned off.

It is important to follow the Manufacturer's instructions while cooking in a microwave as each unit is different.

It is equally necessary to follow cooking instructions on a product label or the instructions for a recipe.

If a time range is given, it is always better to start with the lowest number of minutes recommended, then increase the time accordingly as to reach a safe internal temperature.

TO BE NOTED

All the Recipes in this Book are for 4 generous servings. If cooking for a smaller or larger number, the quantities should be adjusted accordingly.

Likewise, the pungency of the dishes could be reduced by adjusting the amount of chillie powder and other seasonings according to individual tastes.

To bake a cake in a microwave oven, we need to set the power level to 100% of total power efficiency. If you have a microwave oven with the convection mode on, then 180 degrees Celsius is the temperature to set for baking a cake. The texture of cake baked in a microwave oven is different to a traditional convection oven. Test if the cake is cooked or cook for few more minutes. Cooking them longer makes them dry, but unlike convection or conventional ovens they don't burn

Caramelization of sugars on the top surface of the cake does not take place in a microwave oven and hence the top of the cake wont brown. This is because all the heat in a microwave is generated *inside* the cake batter. If the batter is light in color, the cake will also have a light color

All recipes in this book are cooked using 900W for high heat in a microwave.

If your microwave has fewer watts you will need to increase the cooking time, accordingly, and if it has more you will need to reduce it.

1. SOME HELPFUL HINTS AND SUGGESTIONS

1. HINTS BEFORE YOU START COOKING!!!

To get the authentic Anglo-Indian Curry taste while using the recipes in this book, use ginger and garlic paste that is ground at home in a blender using fresh root ginger and garlic. The ready to use ginger and garlic paste available in stores around the world contain vinegar / acetic acid and other preservatives. These detract from the original taste of the Curry giving it a completely different flavour.

If fresh homemade ginger and garlic paste is not available, then Garlic Powder could be used instead of fresh garlic. One teaspoon of garlic powder is equal to one whole garlic, so half a teaspoon would suffice. Ginger powder too can be substituted for fresh ginger. One teaspoon of dry ginger powder mixed with a quarter cup of water is equal to two teaspoons of fresh ginger paste, so half a teaspoon of ginger powder would be equal to one teaspoon of fresh ginger paste.

Any good cooking oil could be used in the preparation of these dishes such as Sun flower Oil, Groundnut Oil or even Olive Oil depending on one's preference.

Always assemble your ingredients and equipment before you start cooking.

Remember to always use fresh ingredients and condiments to get the best taste.

Use very small amounts of water while cooking vegetables in a microwave oven. Vegetables cook fast and the water will take long to evaporate.

Always scrape the skins of the vegetables. Do not peel them, since peeling steals the vitamins from it.

Whole Coriander seeds, cumin seeds, spices, aniseed, red chilies, fenugreek seeds etc., should be heated for a few minutes in the microwave oven before grinding or powdering them. When cooled they become crisp and grind easily.

To skin tomatoes, blanch them in hot water for a few minutes. When slightly cold remove the skins and puree them.

Keep masala powders ready at all time to avoid unnecessary labour and time spent in grinding them when required.

Desiccated coconut can be substituted for fresh coconut. 3 tablespoons of desiccated coconut are equal to ½ cup of fresh grated coconut.

Last but not least a few hints on safety. Always hold the knife with the blade pointing downwards and cut away from you never towards you while cutting meat and vegetables.

Use a potholder or cloth to hold hot dishes when removing them from the Microwave Oven.

2. HOW TO THAW FROZEN MEAT IN A MICROWAVE OVEN

1. Remove food from its packaging before defrosting. Place in a microwave safe dish. Foam trays and plastic wraps are not heat stable at high temperatures and may cause melting or warping from the heat, which could cause harmful chemicals to be released from it into the food.

2. Select the "Defrost" setting or 30% power if your Microwave Oven does not have a separate Defrost Setting.

3. Set the cooking timer. Most meats, such as chicken, beef or pork thaw or defrost in 8 to10 minutes. The thawing time for fish or other seafood can vary, so check the packaging for more information. If your microwave has options for defrosting by weight or defrosting specific foods, use them for best results. Do not leave any meat unattended in the microwave while defrosting

4. During microwave defrosting, rotate and turn food upside down a few times. Stop the timer every few minutes to turn or flip the meat. This helps ensure even thawing.

5. Remove the meat from the microwave and cook immediately after defrosting, as some areas of the frozen food may begin to cook during the defrosting time. Do not hold partially cooked food to use later. You can refreeze your food once cooking is complete.

3. HOW TO DEFROST FRUIT AND VEGETABLES IN THE MICROWAVE

1. Remove your vegetables or fruit from the freezer. Check the weight of the produce or weigh it using kitchen scales.

2. Place your produce in a microwave safe container.

3. Use your microwave's defrost setting or set it to cook at 20-30 percent power.

4. Set the timer for 1 minute and microwave. Turn them over and microwave for one more minute. Most vegetables or fruit defrost within this time.

5. Check the packaging for more information. If your microwave has options for defrosting vegetables or fruits by weight, use them for best results. Check and stir the produce, then repeat until it is completely thawed.

6. Separate pieces out as much as possible. For frozen items such as cooked spinach, pull or squeeze the block apart into smaller pieces and cook immediately.

4. SOME TIPS ON REHEATING COOKED FOOD SAFELY IN THE MICROWAVE

The Microwave is very useful to reheat cooked food. It can revive leftovers in a matter of minutes. Almost any food could be reheated with great results. However, the microwave doesn't heat up food like an oven where the air is heated up to ensure even heating.

In a microwave oven, the microwaves pass through the container of food and stimulate the molecules in the food which then generates heat. This is the reason why microwaved foods cool down faster.

1. Place the food to be reheated in a microwave safe bowl or plate

2. It is always advisable to cover the dish with a lid or a microwave-safe plastic wrap to hold in moisture for safe even heating. Leave a corner of the plastic wrap open for the steam to escape to avoid bursting.

3. Always heat ready-to-eat foods such as hot dogs, luncheon meats, fully cooked ham, and leftovers until steaming hot.

4. After reheating foods in the microwave oven, allow standing time, before consuming.

5. To reheat cooked rice from the fridge, sprinkle a couple teaspoons of water, cover the rice, and microwave for about 30 seconds to one minute. (For every cup of rice to reheat use 2 teaspoons of water)

6. Some food items such as breads, pizza, fries, and other crispy, crumb coated foods like chicken nuggets, fish fingers, etc., either turn dry or soggy if reheated in a microwave. Place a paper towel or napkin between your plate and the slice of pizza, it will absorb excess oils and moisture that usually would result in a soggy slice. Then, place it in your microwave and heat for 1 minute for a steaming hot slice!

7. To reheat a bowl of soup, cover the bowl with a damp paper towel and microwave for 2 minutes, stopping every 60 seconds to stir it. Microwave for 60 seconds more if not heated enough

8. To avoid your Pasta or Noodles, from becoming hard and dry, pour a tablespoon of water or oil over the dish and cover with a paper napkin or microwave lid. Microwave on high for 60 seconds. (Microwave for 30 seconds more if not heated enough)

9. When reheating any type of meat dish, spread the meat equally throughout the dish, so that it heats evenly without cold spots. Cover, the dish with a paper napkin or microwave lid. Microwave on high for 2 minutes initially. Let it rest for a minute, then Microwave for 30 seconds or more if not heated enough.

Reheating meat for less time initially ensures that the texture of the meat does not turn chewy or tough.

10. Baked items or cakes should be reheated in a microwave for very little time. Start with 30 seconds initially then increase by 10 seconds if desired

11. Food should always be reheated up to 75 degrees Celsius. Therefore, the food to be reheated should be placed in a shallow dish and heated on high for 2 minutes initially. Then removed and stirred before heating again for more time, to ensure that there are no cold spots in the food. When the container is opened, steam should come out. That way the desired 75 degrees Celsius would be reached.

12. To heat up or reheat Milk or liquids in the microwave, use a microwave safe cup or container and heat on medium temperature for 30 seconds initially and gradually increasing the time by 10 seconds or so, until it starts to steam. Baby Formula or Breast Milk should never be heated in a microwave

5. CONTAINERS OR WRAPS THAT ARE SAFE TO USE IN THE MICROWAVE

Always use cookware that is specially manufactured for use in the microwave oven. Glass, ceramic containers, and all plastics that are safe to use, would invariably be labelled for microwave oven use.

1. Heatproof glass (such as Pyrex, Anchor Hocking, etc.)

2. Glass-ceramic (such as Corning Ware)

3. Certain type of microwave safe plastic dishes

4. Oven cooking bags.

5. Baskets (straw and wood) for quick warm-ups of rolls or bread. Always Line the basket with either cloth or paper napkins to absorb moisture from the food that is being reheated.

6. Paper plates, towels, napkins and bags could be used, but preferably use white, unprinted materials.

7. Wax paper, parchment paper and heavy plastic wrap.

8. While using plastic wrap to cover food, ensure it does not touch the food. Always leave a corner open to all it to allow steam to escape.

CONTAINERS OR WRAPS THAT ARE NOT SAFE TO USE:

1. Cold storage containers, tubs, cartons, etc. These materials are not approved for cooking and chemicals can seep into the food.

2. Brown paper bags and newspapers.

3. Metal dishes or bowls and Aluminum foil, are a fire hazard if used in the microwave and should never be used as they could create sparks.

4. Foam-insulated cups, bowls, plates or trays.

5. Glass or China Bowls or cups with metallic paint or trim or any containers with metal handles.

6. CLEANING THE INSIDE OF A MICROWAVE OVEN

1. Cleaning your Microwave is literally as simple as microwaving a cup of water for about five minutes. Microwave a cup of water for 5 to 6 minutes. When it's done, the inside of the Oven should be nice and steamy. This makes wiping out the grime inside easier. Remove spatters and spills in your Microwave as they occur so food residue won't become dried on.

2. To clean your microwave, put a solution of 2 tablespoons of baking soda / soda bicarbonate in a cup of water in a (microwave safe) container and cook on high for 2-3 minutes. Remove the container, and then wipe down the microwave's damp interior with a damp paper towel.

3. Baking soda also makes a great stain remover when used in tandem with other substances, such as lemon juice and vinegar. Simply mix the lemon juice and vinegar with the baking soda / powder until they become a paste, and apply to the surface using a soft scrubber or wash cloth. Then clean with warm soapy water (any mild soap or dish washing liquid) and a soft cloth.

4. Remove all traces of soap with a clean damp cloth. Leave the door open for about half an hour before using the Microwave Oven.

5. Do not use steel wool, scouring pads, abrasive cleaners, or oven cleaners.

6. Consult the manufacturer's User Manual for the best advice for your model of microwave oven. Some manufacturers recommend unplugging the microwave before cleaning it to minimize the possibility of electric shock. If you can't locate the manual, follow the above general instructions.

2. STEAMING VEGETABLES IN A MICROWAVE

1. HOW TO STEAM OR BOIL POTATOES IN THE MICROWAVE

Take 2 medium sized potatoes with skins and place them on the microwave turntable. Do not to peel them.

Place a glass or cup of water in the center of the turntable. This is to avoid the potatoes from being wrinkled.

Microwave on high for about 3 minutes.

Turn the potatoes once and microwave for 4 minutes.

Remove the potatoes from microwave, peel and use them.

You can chop them, grate them or mash them as per the recipe.

Alternately, if you don't want to keep the glass or cup of water, to steam potatoes in microwave, you can just prick the potatoes with a sharp knife or fork at intervals. then place them in the microwave and cook.

2. HOW TO STEAM BROCOLLI IN THE MICROWAVE

Chop Broccoli and rinse in salt water
Place the chopped broccoli in a microwave-safe bowl

Add 3 tablespoons of water and shake the dish so that the water trickles down to the bottom of the bowl

Cover with a plate or lid and microwave on high for 3 to 4 minutes, until broccoli is tender.
Carefully remove plate or lid as the steam will be hot

Transfer broccoli to a serving dish and serve plain or toss with butter and a little salt and pepper.

3. HOW TO STEAM CARROTS IN THE MICROWAVE

Peel around 500 grams carrots and chop them into bite-size pieces.

Place them in a microwave-safe bowl
Add 3 tablespoons of water and shake the dish so that the water trickles down to the bottom of the bowl

Cover bowl with a microwave-safe plate or lid and microwave on high for 4 to 5 minutes.

Let carrots sit for one minute before removing the plate, being very careful as steam trapped inside the bowl will be hot.

If you need softer carrots, microwave for one minute more

Once the carrots are cooked, pour off any leftover water

Use the carrots for any dish that calls for steamed carrots.

Alternately, you could add 1 or 2 teaspoons of butter to the steamed carrots, and season with salt, pepper, and / or any herbs

4. HOW TO STEAM FRESH PEAS IN THE MICROWAVE

Place 1 cup of fresh peas in a microwave safe bowl

Add 1or 2 tablespoons of water and shake the dish so that the water trickles down to the bottom of the bowl

Cover with plate and microwave on high for
4 minutes
Remove, mix well, microwave for another
1 minute

Carefully remove plate (the steam will be hot)
Drain away excess water. Use as required in any dish.

Alternately, mix in a teaspoon of butter and season with salt and pepper, enjoy!

To Steam Frozen Peas in the Microwave
Follow the same procedure as above, but microwave only for 1-2 minutes.

5. HOW TO STEAM CAULIFLOWER IN THE MICROWAVE

Wash a whole head of cauliflower well, and cut it into bite-sized florets.

Place the cauliflower florets in a microwave-safe bowl
Add 3 tablespoons of water and shake the dish so that the water trickles down to the bottom of the bowl
Place a microwave plate or lid over the bowl and microwave on high for 3 to 4 minutes. If you need it to be softer, microwave for 1minute more.

Let the cauliflower sit in the microwave for 1 minute before removing from the microwave. Be careful, the steam trapped under the plate will be hot!
Your steamed cauliflower is now ready to be used in any dish that calls for steamed or boiled cauliflower

Alternately, it could be served as a simple side dish, with a little butter or olive oil and salt, or cheese sauce

6. HOW TO STEAM GREEN BEANS IN A MICROWAVE

Wash and trim around 300 grams green beans Place the washed and trimmed green beans in a microwave-safe bowl.

Add 3 tablespoons of water and shake the dish so that the water trickles down to the bottom of the bowl

Cover bowl with a plate and microwave for 4 to 5 minutes, until green beans are tender.

Carefully remove plate as the steam will be hot. Drain away the excess water

Your steamed beans are now ready to be used in any dish that calls for steamed or boiled beans

Alternately, enjoy it by adding a tab of butter. Toss to coat well and sprinkle with salt and pepper.

7. HOW TO STEAM SPINACH OR GREENS IN A MICROWAVE

Rinse around 2 cups of the spinach leaves and drain

Place the spinach or any other greens in a microwave-safe bowl while they are still wet. (If the leaves are still wet, there is no need for additional water)

Cover with a microwave-safe lid or a piece of plastic wrap. Leave one corner of the plastic wrap open to allow moisture to escape during cooking.

Microwave spinach on high for 3 minutes, until all the leaves have turned dark green and are fully wilted.

Season with salt

8. HOW TO STEAM CABBAGE IN A MICROWAVE

Rinse around 2 cups of shredded cabbage and drain

Place the shredded cabbage in a microwave-safe dish

Add 3 tablespoons of water and shake the dish so that the water trickles down to the bottom of the bowl

Cover with a microwave-safe lid or a piece of plastic wrap. Leave one corner of the plastic wrap open to allow moisture to escape during cooking. Microwave on high for 5 minutes.

Drain the water from the dish.

Your steamed cabbage is now ready to be used in any dish that calls for steamed cabbage

Alternately, enjoy it by adding butter and salt or any other seasoning

9. HOW TO STEAM ASPARAGUS IN THE MICROWAVE

Wash and trim the asparagus. If desired, chop each spear in half

Place the spears in a large microwave safe bowl
Add 2 tablespoons of water
Cover the bowl with a microwave safe plate or lid

Microwave on high for 3 minutes until the asparagus is tender but still crisp.

Microwave for 1 minute more if you need it more tender

Carefully remove plate as the steam will be hot.

Use the steamed asparagus as desired or use these options for serving:

1.Drizzle it with melted butter and sprinkle with salt, pepper, and garlic powder.

2. Make a quick dressing of 1 tablespoon olive oil, 1 tablespoon white wine vinegar or lemon juice, a pinch of salt, pepper and a teaspoon of Dijon mustard. Whisk the dressing and then drizzle it over the asparagus.

3. Chop the asparagus and use it in this tasty asparagus salad.

4. Serve it with Hollandaise sauce.

10. HOW TO STEAM BEETROOT IN THE MICROWAVE

2 cups of washed, peeled and cubed beetroots.

Place the beetroot cubes in a microwave safe bowl or dish

Add 2 tablespoons of water

Cover with a microwave-safe lid or a piece of plastic wrap. Leave one corner of the plastic wrap open to allow moisture to escape during cooking.

Microwave on high for 6 minutes. Stir, then microwave for another 2 minutes

Allow to sit covered so they can finish cooking in their steam.

Drain the water from the dish.

Your steamed beetroot is now ready to be used in any dish that calls for steamed beetroot

Alternately, enjoy it by adding a dash of lime and salt or any other seasoning

11. HOW TO MICROWAVE CORN ON THE COB

Trim any excess corn silk and husk from the corn.

Rinse the corn, husk still intact, under running water and place in the microwave. Cook on high for 4 minutes on high.

When corn is cooked, allow the corn to cool slightly and peel the husk. The corn silk and husk should peel easily.

Note: If cooking more than one ear of corn in the microwave at once, add two minutes to the cooking time for each additional ear of corn

12. HOW TO MICROWAVE MIXED VEGETABLES

If you're using bigger veggies or a mixture of different types, cut them into manageable pieces of roughly the same size.

Place them into a microwave-safe dish. Add 2 tablespoons of water (a little more if you're steaming multiple portions).

Place in the microwave. Cover them with a triple layer of damp paper towels.

Microwave on high heat for 5 to 6 minutes or until the vegetables are tender

3. HOW TO BOIL EGGS IN A MICROWAVE

Take a microwave safe bowl and add water that is enough to submerge the eggs (It should be around ½ inch above the eggs). Microwave on high for 3 minutes until hot.

Lightly prick the bottom of each egg with a safety pin to prevent the egg from exploding while boiling

Place the eggs carefully into the bowl or dish of hot water

Add ½ teaspoon of salt for each egg such as 1 teaspoon for 2 eggs and 3 teaspoons for 6 eggs to the water

Cover with a plate. Microwave at 50% power for 4 minutes

If you want soft boiled eggs with runny egg yolks, remove the eggs from the hot water and plunge them immediately into a bowl of cold water.

If you want hard boiled eggs, allow them to stay in the hot water for 2 to 3 more minutes. Two minutes will give you just slightly creamy egg yolks.

Three minutes will give you firm egg yolks.

These boiled eggs could be used for any dish calling for hard boiled eggs

4. BREAKFAST IN A JIFFY

1. TWO MINUTE SCRAMBLED EGGS

Ingredients:
2 eggs
2 tablespoons milk
Salt, pepper, and any other herbs of your choice
for seasoning

Method

Beat the eggs and milk and beat till well blended

Add the salt, pepper and seasoning and mix in

Coat a small microwave safe mug or dish with oil
or cooking spray

Pour the egg and milk mixture into this bowl

Microwave on high for 1 minute.

Remove and stir the mixture to break it up

Microwave for I minute more or until eggs are
almost set

Leave it as it is or break it up into small chunks

Enjoy it with buttered toast

2. SCRAMBLED EGGS WITH ONIONS

Ingredients:
2 eggs
2 tablespoons milk
1 small onion chopped finely
1 green chillie chopped
Salt, pepper, and any other herbs of your choice
for seasoning

Method

Beat the eggs and milk and beat till well blended

Add the salt, pepper and seasoning and mix in
the chopped onions and green chillies

Coat a small microwave dish with oil or cooking
spray

Pour the egg and milk mixture into this bowl

Microwave on high for 1 minute.

Remove and stir the mixture to break it up
Microwave for I minute more or until eggs are
almost set

Leave it as it is or break it up into small chunks

Enjoy it with buttered toast

3. FRIED EGG

Ingredients
1 Egg
1 tablespoon oil
Salt and pepper to taste

Method

Coat a small microwave safe mug or dish with 1 tablespoon oil or cooking spray

Crack an egg into the bowl and poke a hole in the egg yolk with a fork or toothpick.

Cover the dish with a microwave-safe lid or cling wrap

Microwave on high for 30 seconds

The yolk would be runny and soft.

Microwave for 30 seconds more if you want a well-cooked yolk

4. OMLETTE WITH ONIONS

Ingredients
2 eggs
2 tablespoons chopped onions
Salt, Pepper or any other herbs or seasoning to taste

Method

Beat the eggs till frothy

Add the salt, pepper and seasoning or herbs and mix in

Coat a small microwave safe dish with one tablespoon oil or cooking spray

Pour the egg into this bowl

Cover the dish with a microwave-safe lid or cling wrap

Microwave on high for 1 minute. Remove and stir

Microwave for 2 more minutes till the omelette is firm

Microwave for 30 seconds more if a firmer omelette is desired

5. POACHED EGGS

Ingredients
1 large egg
¼ teaspoon white vinegar
1/3 cup water
Salt and pepper

Method

Add the water and white vinegar to a ramekin or custard cup.

Break the egg into cup

Now pierce egg yolk with toothpick and cover dish loosely with plastic wrap or a lid

Microwave on high for 1 minute or 30 seconds more is you want the yolk firmer.

Immediately remove the egg from the hot water with a slotted spoon.

Sprinkle salt and pepper to taste

6. EGG FRITATA

Ingredients

3 eggs beaten well
2 tablespoons oil or butter
2 tablespoons finely chopped green or red bell pepper / capsicums
3 tablespoons fine chopped mushrooms
1 medium size onion chopped finely
2 small tomatoes roughly chopped
3 tablespoons grated Parmesan Cheese
1 teaspoon crushed or ground black pepper and any other dried herbs or seasoning as desired
3 tablespoons chopped ham or spam (optional)
Salt to taste
½ cup milk
2 tablespoons fresh chopped coriander leaves for garnish

Method

Beat the eggs and milk till well combined

Add the salt, pepper and seasoning or herbs and mix in and keep aside

Coat a microwave safe dish with 2 tablespoons oil or butter

Lay the chopped onions, tomatoes, green / red peppers and mushrooms at the bottom of the bowl

Top this with the chopped ham or spam

Pour the beaten eggs into the dish and shake the dish gently so that it covers the bottom layer of chopped veggies. Spread the grated cheese on top

Cover the dish with a microwave-safe lid or cling wrap

Microwave on high for 2 minutes or 30 seconds more if you require it more firm

Once the Frittata is perfectly cooked, remove it from the microwave oven.

Garnish with chopped spring onion or coriander leaves. Serve it hot in wedges or as an individual dish along with fried sausages or bacon.

7. HAM AND EGGS

Ingredients
3 eggs beaten well
2 tablespoons oil or butter
2 small tomatoes roughly chopped
2 tablespoons fresh chopped chives or spring onions for garnish
Salt, pepper and any other dried herbs or seasoning as desired
3 tablespoons chopped ham or spam (optional)
½ cup milk

Method

Beat the eggs well. Add the chopped ham, tomatoes, chives / spring onions, salt, pepper and seasoning or herbs and mix in and keep aside

Coat a microwave safe dish with 2 tablespoons oil or butter

Pour the beaten eggs into the dish

Spread some grated cheese on top if desired

Cover the dish with a microwave-safe lid or cling wrap

Microwave on high for 2 minutes and 30 seconds till the eggs are firm

Garnish with chopped spring onion or chives

8. FRENCH TOAST IN A MUG

Ingredients
2 large eggs
½ cup milk
1 teaspoon vanilla essence or extract
½ teaspoon cinnamon powder
1 tablespoon softened butter
4 slices sandwich bread broken into small bits
1 tablespoon raisins
2 tablespoons chopped nuts of your choice

Method
Beat the eggs, milk, vanilla essence and cinnamon together
Coat 3 microwave safe mugs or cups with butter or oil spray
Divide the bread chunks between the 3 mugs. Gently pour the milk and egg mixture over the bread in the 3 mugs
Top each mug with raisins and chopped nuts
Microwave on high for 1 minute and 30 seconds till milk and mixture sets.

Serve warm with powdered cinnamon sugar or maple syrup

9. CINNAMON MUFFINS

Ingredients
8 tablespoons Flour
2 eggs beaten
½ teaspoon baking powder
½ cup milk
2 tablespoon vegetable oil or butter

2 tablespoons sugar
1 teaspoon vanilla essence or extract
¼ teaspoon salt
1 teaspoon cinnamon powder

Method
Mix all the ingredients together till well combined

Grease 4 ramekins or a microwave safe muffin tray and spoon in the batter. Microwave on high for 3 minutes

Check if the insides are cooked by inserting a toothpick. If not done, microwave for 1 minute more

10. OATS PORRIDGE IN A JIFFY

Ingredients
½ cup breakfast oats or rolled oats
½ cup milk
½ cup water

Method
Mix the oats, water and milk together in a large microwave safe bowl to avoid spilling over when cooking.
Microwave uncovered on high power for 2 minutes. Remove and stir.
Microwave for 2 more minutes. Repeat if necessary until it boils and thickens, and becomes smooth and creamy.
Add sugar or your favourite toppings such as sliced banana, sultanas, canned or fresh fruit, chopped dates, or more milk

5. MICROWAVE SOUPS RECIPES

Thick meat or vegetable soups are ideal "filler ups" when you don't feel like having a huge meal or when not feeling well. Soup cubes readily available in the shops can be added to enhance the flavour of the soup made at home. Soup made from leftover meat bones when cooked with a few vegetables and salt and pepper would taste heavenly!!!!!!!!!!!!!!!!

Here are some easy recipes to make your favourite soups in minutes in the Microwave Oven

1. POTATO AND LEEK SOUP

Ingredients
1 cup chopped onion leeks
1cup peeled and cubed potatoes
3 tablespoons butter
2 cups chicken stock or warm water
1 cup milk
¼ cup cream
Salt and Pepper to season

Method

Place the leeks, potatoes and butter in a fairly large microwave safe bowl.
Cover the dish with a lid with holes or plastic wrap, leaving one side unsealed for venting
Microwave on high for 3 minutes
Remove and gradually add the stock / warm water, pepper and salt
Re-cover the dish and microwave on high for 12 minutes with 3-minute rests in between. Stir well each time
Check if the potatoes and leeks are cooked, otherwise microwave on high for 2 minutes more
Leave aside to cool slightly.
Place in a liquidizer and blend until smooth.
Stir in the cream and season to taste.

Heat on medium heat for 3 mins or until piping hot before serving

2. CREAM OF TOMATO SOUP

Ingredients:
3 large ripe tomatoes chopped
1 onion chopped
½ teaspoon chopped garlic
2 cups warm water or vegetable stock
Salt and Pepper to taste
½ teaspoon sugar
2 tablespoons butter
½ cup cream

Method

Put the butter, garlic and onions in a large microwave safe bowl and microwave on high for 3 minutes
Remove and add the chopped tomatoes to the bowl
Cover with a lid with holes or plastic wrap, leaving one side unsealed for venting
Microwave on high for 3 minutes
Remove and gradually add the stock / warm water, sugar, pepper and salt
Re-cover the dish and microwave on high for 12 minutes with 3-minute rests in between. Stir well each time
Leave aside to cool slightly.
Add the cream and mix well
Place in a liquidiser and blend until smooth
Add more seasoning if necessary
Heat on medium heat for 3 mins or until piping hot before serving
Garnish with a dash of cream and a sprig of mint

3. SWEET CORN CHICKEN SOUP

Ingredients
1 can sweet corn
2 cups water
3 cups chicken stock
½ cup boiled and shredded chicken
2 tablespoons cornflour (mix in 1/2 cup water)
Salt and pepper to taste

Method

Place the chicken stock and shredded chicken in a large microwave safe bowl
Cover the dish with a lid with holes or plastic wrap, leaving one side unsealed for venting
Microwave on high for 5 minutes, with 3-minute rests
Leave aside
Place the sweet corn and 2 cups of water in another microwave safe bowl
Cover with a lid with holes or plastic wrap, leaving one side unsealed for venting
Microwave on high for 6 minutes, with 3-minute rests
Now transfer the cooked sweet corn to the already microwaved chicken stock and chicken and add salt and pepper to taste.
Mix the corn flour with half cup cold water and add to the chicken and corn. Mix well
Microwave covered on high for 3 minutes.
Let it stand for 2 minutes.
Serve hot.

4. SPINACH SOUP

Ingredients
3 cups of chopped spinach
2 tablespoons all-purpose flour
2 tablespoons butter
½ cup milk
2 tablespoons fresh cream
Salt and Pepper to taste

Method
Place the spinach leaves in a microwave safe dish and microwave on high for 2 or 3 minutes or till the spinach gets well cooked
Set aside to cool
Blend the cooled spinach till well pureed
Add the butter to another big microwave bowl and microwave on high for 30 seconds
Add the all-purpose flour and some milk and mix well till smooth
Add the spinach puree, the rest of the milk, salt and pepper and mix well
Cover the dish with a lid with holes or plastic wrap, leaving one side unsealed for venting
Microwave on high for 4 minutes with 2-minute rests (stir it once after 2 mins)
Garnish with fresh cream

5. CARROT SOUP

Ingredients
2 tablespoons butter
1 large onion, chopped
2 cups peeled and chopped carrots
1 teaspoon chopped garlic

1 teaspoon dried thyme
2 cups vegetable stock
Salt and Pepper to taste
4 tablespoons heavy cream
½ teaspoon Paprika (optional)
Some chopped spring onion to garnish

Method
Add the butter, onions and garlic in a large microwave safe bowl and microwave on high for 2 minutes
Add carrots, garlic, dried thyme and stock and mix together
Cover the dish with a lid with holes or plastic wrap, leaving one side unsealed for venting
Microwave on high for 12 minutes with 3-minute rests, or till the carrots are tender. (Stirring each time)
Set aside to cool
Blend the cooled carrots till well pureed
Season with salt and pepper
Garnish with a sprinkle of paprika and fresh chopped spring onions

6. MINESTRONE SOUP

Ingredients
1 onion, chopped
½ teaspoon chopped garlic
1 cup each chopped carrots
½ cup chopped celery
2 tablespoons oil
1 can beef stock or broth
1 can diced tomatoes
1 teaspoon dried basil or mint

Salt and pepper to taste

Method

Add the oil, onions, garlic, carrots, celery in a large microwave safe bowl
Cover the dish with a lid with holes or plastic wrap, leaving one side unsealed for venting
Microwave on high for 3-minutes
Add all the other remaining minutes
Cover and microwave on high for 12 minutes with 3-minute rests in
between, or till the veggies are tender. (Stirring each time)
Season with salt and pepper
Garnish with shredded cheese

7. BROCCOLI AND CHEESE SOUP

Ingredients
1 cup broccoli florets
2 tablespoons all-purpose flour
2 tablespoons butter
½ cup milk
2 cups warm water
1 cup shredded cheddar cheese
1 soup cube any flavour of your choice
Salt and pepper to taste

Method

Place the broccoli with 2 tablespoons of water in a microwave safe bowl
Cover the dish with a lid with holes or plastic wrap, leaving one side unsealed for venting
Microwave on high for 3 minutes till the broccoli is tender

Meanwhile, combine the flour, soup cube, salt, pepper and milk till smooth.
Mix this with the steamed broccoli
Add the warm water and mix well
Cover and microwave on high for 6 minutes, with 3-minute rests in
between. (Stirring each time)
Remove and stir in the cheese until melted.
Season with salt and pepper to taste
Serve hot

8. CREAMY VEGETABLE SOUP

Ingredients
½ cup peeled and cubed potatoes
½ cup diced carrots
½ cup green peas
½ cup sweet corn
¼ cup chopped spring onions
½ teaspoon chopped and crushed garlic or garlic powder
1 cup vegetable or chicken stock (or warm water)
½ cup milk
1 tablespoon cornflour or corn starch
Salt and Pepper to taste
3 tablespoons grated cheddar cheese or any cheese of your choice

Method

Place the potato cubes and carrots in a microwave safe bowl with 3 tablespoons of water.
Microwave on high for 3 minutes
Remove and add in the garlic, peas, sweet corn, milk, ½ cup stock or water and mix in the corn flour

Cover the dish with a lid with holes or plastic
wrap, leaving one side unsealed for venting
Microwave on high for 6 minutes, with 3-minute
rests in between. (Stirring each time)
Remove and stir in the cheese until melted.
Season with salt and pepper to taste
Garnish with chopped spring onions
Serve hot

9. EGG AND VEGETABLE MUG SOUP

Ingredients
2 tablespoons chopped carrot
1 tablespoon chopped celery
1 soup cube (any flavour of your choice)
¾ water or just enough to cover the vegetables
1 egg

Method

Place the chopped carrot, celery in a large mug
Add the soup cube and water, making sure to
leave one inch space to the top of the mug

Microwave on high for 4 minutes with 2-minute
rests in between. (Stirring each time). Make sure
that the soup does not boil over.

Remove and crack egg into mug, then stir gently.
Make sure to break open the yolk.

Microwave again on for 2 minutes, to make sure
that the egg is cooked
Serve hot

10. LEMON CORIANDER MUG SOUP

Ingredients

3 tablespoons fresh roughly chopped coriander
1 tablespoon lemon juice
¼ teaspoon finely chopped ginger
¼ teaspoon chopped and crushed garlic
1 small green chillie sliced
1 teaspoon corn starch / corn flour
Salt and pepper to taste
¾ cup vegetable stock or water

Method

Mix the corn flour / corn starch with a little water and keep aside
Place the chopped coriander, garlic, ginger and green chillie in a large mug
Add the vegetable stock or water, making sure to leave one inch space to the top of the mug

Microwave on high for 4 minutes with 2-minute rests in between. (Stirring each time). Make sure that the soup does not boil over

Remove and mix in the corn flour / starch mixture

Microwave again on for 2 minutes

Add the lemon / lime juice, salt and pepper to taste and mix well
Serve hot

6. MICROWAVE MULLIGATWANY SOUP RECIPES

Mulligatawny Soup is the anglicized version of the Tamil word "Melligu -Thani" meaning Pepper and Water. During colonial times it became very popular with the British and the Anglo–Indians. However, in order to suit their delicate palates, the pungency of the soup was reduced. In course of time a lot of other ingredients such coconut, meat, poultry and spices were added to give it a completely different flavour. The dish quickly became popular throughout the colonies of the Common Wealth. The Mulligatawny Soup of today bears little resemblance to the original "MELLIGU -THANI".

Mulligatawny Soup is a creamy, curried soup. This heart-warming soup could be prepared with or without lentils, meat or chicken. There are many recipes for Mulligatawny with different ingredients. Mulligatawny Soup is easy to make and is delicious and flavourful with a slight spicy-tangy taste. It is an excellent "Comfort" dish on a cold rainy day and will surely lift the spirits when one is down in the dumps.

This hearty soup could be served as a lunch or dinner meal, with bread rolls and a side salad to round it out. Any left-overs could be frozen and enjoyed at a later date by reheating it in the microwave

1. RED LENTIL MULLIGATAWNY SOUP

Ingredients
3 tablespoon cooked basmati rice or any raw rice
3 tablespoons red lentils (masur dal) or any lentils of your choice (or use
canned chickpeas instead)
1 teaspoon red chilli powder
1 teaspoon coriander powder
½ teaspoon turmeric powder
1 teaspoon crushed pepper
1 teaspoon cumin powder
½ teaspoon garam masala powder or spice powder
2 tablespoons butter or ghee
½ cup Coconut milk
1 bay leaf
1 teaspoon tamarind paste
1 teaspoon ginger garlic paste
1 large finely chopped onion
Salt to taste

Method

Soak the lentils in water for one hour before cooking
Add the butter, bay leaf and onions in a microwave safe bowl
Cover the dish with a lid with holes or plastic wrap, leaving one side unsealed for venting
Microwave on high for 3-minutes
Add the lentils and all the other ingredients to the bowl and mix well.

Cover the dish and Microwave on high for 6 minutes

Remove and mix in 2 cups of water or vegetable stock.

Microwave again on high for 5 minutes.

Remove and add the cooked Rice and mix well

Microwave on high for 2 minutes

Serve hot with a dash of lime juice

2. CHICKEN MULLIGATAWNY SOUP WITHOUT LENTILS

Ingredients

½ kg chicken breast cut into bite size cubes

2 cups chicken stock

1 cup cooked rice

1 carrot shredded

1 potato peeled and shredded

1 apple peeled and diced (use any tart apple such as granny smith etc)

1teaspoon chilli powder

1 teaspoon crushed pepper or pepper powder

1teaspoon cumin powder

1teaspoon coriander powder

1teaspoon crushed garlic

2 big onions sliced

2 cloves

2 small pieces cinnamon

2 Bay leaves

2 tablespoons oil or butter

1 cup coconut paste or coconut milk

Salt to taste

Marinate the chicken with the chilli powder, crushed pepper or pepper powder, cumin powder, coriander powder and salt for one hour

Add the butter, crushed garlic, bay leaf, cinnamon, cloves and onions in a microwave safe bowl

Cover the dish with a lid with holes or plastic wrap, leaving one side unsealed for venting

Microwave on high for 3-minutes

Remove and add the marinated chicken, shredded carrots, potato and apple and mix in.

Cover and microwave on high for 3 minutes

Remove and mix in the chicken stock

Cover the dish and Microwave on high for 6 minutes

Check if the chicken is cooked or else microwave on high for a few more minutes

Remove and add the coconut milk and the cooked Rice and mix well

Microwave on high for 3 minutes more

Garnish with chopped coriander or parsley

Serve hot with a sliver of lemon and bread rolls

3. CHICKEN AND LENTILS MULLIGATAWNY SOUP

Ingredients

500 grams boneless chicken

½ cup red (masur dal) or yellow lentils (moong dal)

2 cups chicken broth

2 tablespoons butter

1 apple peeled and chopped into pieces

1 large onion sliced

1 teaspoon chopped garlic

1 teaspoon curry powder

½ teaspoon garam masala
1 cup coconut milk
2 tablespoons fresh lemon juice
2 cups cooked basmati rice
Lemon wedges to garnish

Method

Soak the lentils in water for one hour before cooking
Marinate the chicken with the curry powder, garam masala powder and salt for one hour
Add the butter, chopped garlic and onions in a microwave safe bowl

Cover the dish with a lid with holes or plastic wrap, leaving one side unsealed for venting

Microwave on high for 3-minutes
Remove and add the marinated chicken, lentils and apple and mix in
Cover and microwave on high for 3 minutes
Remove and mix in the chicken broth or stock

Cover the dish and Microwave on high for 6 minutes. Check if the chicken is cooked or else microwave on high for a few more minutes

Remove and add the coconut milk and mix well
Microwave on high for 3 minutes more
Mix in the lime juice and leave to cool a bit
Divide the rice among bowls. Pour the soup over the rice.

Garnish with lemon wedges and Serve

4. LAMB / MUTTON MULLIGATAWNY SOUP

Ingredients
½ kg lamb or mutton (beef if preferred), cut into small pieces
½ cup Red Gram Lentils (Masoor Dal)
2 cups coconut milk
2 tablespoons oil
2 cups of any stock or broth
1 teaspoon red chilli powder
1 teaspoon coriander powder
½ teaspoon turmeric powder
1 teaspoon cumin powder
1 teaspoon ground pepper / pepper powder
1 tablespoon ginger garlic paste
2 tablespoons lime juice
Salt to taste
1 large onion sliced finely
8 to 10 curry leaves
3 green chilies
2 medium size potatoes peeled and diced into small cubes
2 tablespoons chopped mint for garnishing

Method

Soak the lentils in water for one hour before cooking

Marinate the meat with the red chilli powder, coriander powder, turmeric
powder, cumin powder, ground pepper / pepper powder, ginger garlic paste
and salt for one hour

Take the oil, onions, curry leaves and green chillies in a large microwave
safe bowl

Cover the dish with a lid with holes or plastic wrap, leaving one side unsealed for venting
Microwave on high for 3-minutes

Remove and add the marinated meat, lentils and potatoes and mix in

Cover and microwave on high for 6 minutes

Remove and add in the broth or stock. Mix well
Cover the dish and Microwave on high for 6 minutes. Check if the meat is cooked or else microwave on high for a few more minutes. Repeat till the meat is tender.

Remove and add the coconut milk and mix well
Microwave on high for 3 minutes more
Mix in the lime juice and leave to cool a bit
Garnish with mint leaves
Serve just as a soup or with bread or rice.

5. BEEF MINCE MULLIGATAWNY SOUP

Ingredients
300 grams Beef Mince / Ground Beef
2 tablespoons butter or oil
1 large onion sliced
1 teaspoon chopped garlic
2 carrots peeled and diced into cubes
1 apple peeled and diced into cubes
2 tablespoons of any curry powder
½ teaspoon ground pepper

3 tablespoons flour (make a paste with ½ cup of water)
3 cups broth or stock or warm water
2 tablespoons chopped fresh or dried mint
1 cup cream
Salt to taste
1 cup cooked rice

Method
Marinate the beef mince with the curry powder, mint, pepper and salt for one hour
Add the butter, chopped garlic and onions in a large microwave safe bowl
Cover the dish with a lid with holes or plastic wrap, leaving one side unsealed for venting
Microwave on high for 3-minutes
Remove and add the marinated beef mince, carrots and apple and mix well
Cover and microwave on high for 5 minutes
Remove and mix in the flour and broth or stock
Cover the dish and Microwave on high for 6 minutes
Check if the mince and carrots are cooked or else microwave on high for a few more minutes
Remove and mash everything well.
Add the 1 more cup of stock or water and mix well
Microwave on high for 3 minutes more
Stir in the cream
Divide the rice among bowls. Pour the soup over the rice.
Garnish with lemon wedges and Serve

7. MICROWAVE PEPPERWATER RECIPES

1. ANGLO-INDIAN PEPPERWATER

Pepper water (more like a South Indian Rasam) invariably forms part of the afternoon meal in Anglo-Indian homes in the South of India on some days.

It is a watery, peppery, tangy concoction, usually had with plain white rice and accompanied by meat, poultry, or a seafood dish that is generally a dry fry.

Pepper water should always be of a watery consistency.

Many people like to drink a cup of pepper water after a meal since it aids in digestion.

Ingredients for the Pepper Water

2 large tomatoes chopped
1 teaspoon pepper powder
½ teaspoon chillie powder
1 teaspoon cumin powder
½ teaspoon turmeric powder
½ teaspoon coriander powder
Salt to taste
½ cup tamarind juice extracted from a small ball of tamarind or 2 teaspoons tamarind paste

Ingredients for the Tempering

I small onion sliced
2 red chilies broken into bits
1 teaspoon chopped garlic crushed roughly

½ teaspoon mustard seeds
A few curry leaves
2 teaspoons oil

Method
Add the oil, onions, garlic, mustard seeds, red chillies and curry leaves in a microwave safe bowl

Cover the dish with a lid with holes or plastic wrap, leaving one side unsealed for venting

Microwave on high for 3-minutes
Remove and keep aside. This is the Tempering

Now take a large microwave safe bowl and mix the chopped tomatoes, pepper powder, chillie powder, cumin powder, turmeric powder, coriander powder, salt to taste and the tamarind juice with 2 cups of water

Cover the dish with a lid with holes or plastic wrap, leaving one side unsealed for venting
Microwave on high for 6 minutes

Remove and add the Tempering that has already been microwaved

Microwave on high for 2 minutes
Serve hot with rice and a side dish

Note: The pepper water could also be prepared by using fresh red chilies, cumin seeds, coriander seeds and peppercorns ground in a mixer or blender instead of the powders.

2. BREAST BONE PEPPER WATER

Ingredients for the Breast Bone Pepper Water:
½ kg soft bones and pieces of meat preferably from the breast portion
(Use either beef, lamb or mutton)
2 teaspoons cumin powder
1 teaspoon chillie powder
1 teaspoon pepper powder
2 teaspoons coriander powder
½ teaspoon turmeric powder
1 large tomato chopped
Salt to taste
1 teaspoon ginger garlic paste
½ cup tamarind juice
½ cup coconut paste or coconut milk (optional)
2 tablespoons chopped coriander leaves for garnishing

Ingredients for the Tempering:
½ teaspoon mustard seeds
2 red chillies broken into bits
A few curry leaves
1 small onion sliced
2 teaspoons oil

Method

Take the oil, mustard seeds, red chillies, curry leaves and onions in a small microwave safe bowl
Cover the dish with a lid with holes or plastic wrap, leaving one side unsealed for venting
Microwave on high for 3-minutes
Remove and keep aside. This is the Tempering

Now take a large microwave safe bowl and add all the above-mentioned ingredients for the Bone Pepper Water (except the coconut milk) along with 2 cups of water
Cover the dish with a lid with holes or plastic wrap, leaving one side unsealed for venting
Microwave on high for 5 minutes. Remove and mix well
Microwave again on high for 10 minutes, with 5-minute rests, stirring each time. Remove and mix well
Remove and add the coconut milk and tempering that has already been microwaved. Mixed well
Microwave on high for 5 minutes more

Garnish with coriander leaves.
Serve hot with plain rice and any vegetable side dish and chutney or pickle

3. DOL (DHAL) PEPPER WATER
(Lentil based Pepper Water)

Ingredients for the Dol Pepperwater
½ cup Red Lentils or Masur Dal
2 cups of water
1 large tomato chopped
½ teaspoon chillie powder
1 teaspoon cumin powder
1 teaspoon pepper powder
½ teaspoon turmeric powder
1 teaspoon coriander powder
½ cup tamarind juice extracted from a small ball of tamarind or 2 teaspoons tamarind paste
Salt to taste

A few coriander leaves to garnish

For the Tempering:
½ teaspoon mustard seeds
2 red chillies broken into bits
A few curry leaves
2 teaspoons oil

Method

Take the oil, mustard seeds, red chillies and curry leaves in a small microwave safe bowl
Cover the dish with a lid with holes or plastic wrap, leaving one side unsealed for venting
Microwave on high for 3-minutes
Remove and keep aside. This is the Tempering

Now take a large microwave safe bowl and add all the above-mentioned ingredients for the Dol Pepper Water along with 3 cups of water
Cover the dish with a lid with holes or plastic wrap, leaving one side unsealed for venting

Microwave on high for 5 minutes. Remove and mix well
Microwave again on high for 5 minutes. Remove and mix well
Remove and add the Tempering that has already been microwaved
Microwave on high for 5 minutes more

Garnish with the chopped coriander leaves

Serve hot with rice and a meat side dish and vegetable foogath

4. TOMATO PEPPERWATER WITHOUT TAMARIND

Ingredients
2 large tomatoes chopped into quarters
1 teaspoon pepper powder
1 teaspoon cumin powder
1 teaspoon crushed garlic
Salt to taste
1 tablespoon chopped coriander leaves
A few Curry leaves

Method

Place the tomatoes with 1 cup of water in a microwave safe bowl
Cover the dish with a lid with holes or plastic wrap, leaving one side
unsealed for venting
Microwave on high for 5 minutes. The tomatoes should have turned to pulp by now
Remove and mash the tomatoes well with a fork or masher. Remove the skins
Add the pepper powder, cumin powder, crushed garlic, Salt, chopped coriander leaves and curry leaves. Mix all well together with 1 more cup of water
Cover the dish with a lid with holes or plastic wrap, leaving one side
unsealed for venting
Microwave on high for 5 to 6 minutes till you see the mixture beginning to get frothy
Garnish with chopped coriander leaves.
Serve as a hot drink or with rice and a side dish

5. MICROWAVE INSTANT PEPPERWATER IN A MUG USING TOMATO PUREE

Ingredients

1 teaspoon tomato puree or tomato paste
½ teaspoon ground pepper
¼ teaspoon cumin powder
1 garlic pearl smashed
1 tablespoon lemon juice
1 tablespoon chopped coriander
3 or 4 curry leaves (optional)
Salt to taste

Method

Place all the above ingredients with 1 cup of water in a large microwave safe mug. Mix well together

Microwave on high heat for 6 minutes

Serve hot

8. MICROWAVE CHICKEN DISHES

1. ANGLO-INDIAN PEPPER CHICKEN

Ingredients
200 grams boneless chicken breast
1 teaspoon crushed black pepper
Salt to taste
2 tablespoons oil

Method

Marinate the chicken with the pepper, salt and oil for two hours
Place the chicken in a Microwave dish

Cover the dish with a lid with holes or plastic wrap, leaving one side unsealed for venting
Cook on high for 5 minutes.
Turn the chicken over to the other side and microwave again for 4 minutes
Check and cook for a little more time until the chicken is properly cooked.

2. PEPPER CHICKEN DRUMSTICKS

Ingredients
6 Chicken Drumsticks with the skin
2 teaspoons crushed black pepper
Salt to taste
3 tablespoons oil

Method

Marinate the chicken with the pepper, salt and oil for 2 hours

Place the chicken in a fan arrangement with the thin parts of the legs in the center of a round microwave dish

Cover the dish with a lid with holes or plastic wrap, leaving one side unsealed for venting

Microwave on high for 5minutes then turn the legs over

Microwave again for 4 to 5 minutes till the chicken is cooked and tender.

3. SIMPLE CHICKEN FRY

Ingredients
500 grams chicken cut into medium size pieces
2 teaspoons ginger garlic paste
3 tablespoons oil
1 teaspoon red chillie powder
1 teaspoon cumin powder
1 piece cinnamon
Salt to taste

Method

Pat each chicken piece dry.
Marinate the chicken with all the above ingredients and refrigerate for 2 to 3 hours or over night
Arrange the chicken in a microwave dish.
Cover the dish with a lid with holes or plastic wrap, leaving one side unsealed for venting
Microwave the chicken for 15 minutes, with 5-minute rests to turn the pieces over to ensure that is has cooked well.
Serve as a side dish

4. ANGLO-INDIAN CHICKEN CURRY

Ingredients
1 kg chicken without the skin, cut into medium size pieces
2 medium size onions sliced
2 medium size tomatoes chopped
2 teaspoons ginger garlic paste
1 teaspoon coriander powder
½ teaspoon turmeric powder

½ teaspoon cumin powder
1 or 2 teaspoons red chillie powder
½ teaspoon garam masala powder
Salt to taste
2 tablespoons chopped coriander leaves
3 tablespoons oil
1 cup water

Method

Mix the chicken with all the ingredients in a large microwave bowl
Refrigerate for 2 hours or more
When ready to cook, remove from the fridge
Cover the dish with a lid with holes or plastic wrap, leaving one side unsealed for venting
Microwave on high for 5 minutes.
Remove and mix well
Microwave again for 5 minutes more till done
Mix in 3 tablespoons coconut milk and microwave for 3 more minutes
Garnish with chopped coriander leaves
Serve with rice or bread

5. ANGLO-INDIAN CHICKEN VINDALOO

Ingredients
500 grams chicken cut into medium pieces
2 big onions chopped
3 medium potatoes peeled and cut into quarters
3 tablespoons oil
1 teaspoon mustard powder or paste
2 teaspoon chillie powder
1 teaspoon cumin powder
2 teaspoons garlic paste
¼ cup vinegar

½ teaspoon turmeric powder
Salt to taste
1 cup water

Method
Mix the chicken with all the ingredients in a large microwave bowl
Refrigerate for 2 hours or more
When ready to cook, remove from the fridge
Cover the dish with a lid
Microwave on high for 6 minutes.
Remove and mix well
Microwave again for 5 minutes more till done
Serve with hoppers, bread, rice or chapattis.

6. CHICKEN COUNTRY CAPTAIN

Ingredients
500 grams chicken cut into medium size pieces
2 large onions sliced
2 bay leaves
1 teaspoon chillie powder
1 teaspoons coriander powder
2 teaspoons ginger garlic paste
Salt to taste
3 tablespoons oil
2 dry red chillies broken into bits
2 cloves
1 piece cinnamon
2 tablespoons milk or cream
1 cup water

Method
Mix the chicken with all the ingredients in a large microwave bowl
Refrigerate for 2 hours or more

When ready to cook, remove from the fridge
Cover the dish with a lid with holes or plastic wrap, leaving one side unsealed for venting
Microwave on high for 5 minutes.
Remove and mix well
Microwave again for 5 minutes
Remove and mix then again microwave for 2 minutes more till done
Serve with rice or bread

7. ANGLO-INDIAN CHICKEN AND POTATO STEW

A hearty and robust Anglo-Indian Chicken and Potato Stew that is both healthy and appetizing

Ingredients
1 chicken weighing around 1 kg cut into medium pieces
2 potatoes peeled and cut into quarters
3 green chilies slit lengthwise
1 medium size tomato chopped
1 big onion sliced
2 teaspoons ginger garlic paste
2 cloves,
2 small pieces of cinnamon,
6 or 7 pepper corns
A few mint leaves
Salt to taste
2 tablespoons oil
1 cup water

Method
Mix the chicken with all the ingredients in a large microwave bowl
Refrigerate for 2 hours or more

When ready to cook, remove from the fridge

Add ½ cup of coconut milk and mix to combine

Cover the dish with a lid with holes or plastic wrap, leaving one side unsealed for venting

Microwave on high for 5 minutes.
Remove and mix well

Microwave again for 5 minutes more till done
Remove and mix in ½ cup of warm water or stock

Microwave for 2 more minutes
Serve hot with bread or hoppers.

8. CHICKEN DEVIL FRY

The term 'Devilled' originated during the time of the British Raj in India. The Colonial servants would recycle the leftover Turkey and Chicken Roasts into a hot Fry or Dry Dish with the addition of some hot seasonings or condiments such as pepper, chillies, etc. Hence the term 'Devilled'. This spicy dish tickles the palate with a burst of flavours.

Ingredients
1 kg chicken cut into medium size pieces or leftover Chicken Roast
3 teaspoons chopped garlic
2 teaspoon chillie powder
3 onions sliced
2 tablespoons tomato sauce or ketchup

Salt to taste
3 green chillies
1 teaspoon pepper powder
1 teaspoon cumin powder
3 tablespoons oil
2 tablespoons vinegar
2 teaspoons Worcestershire sauce
2 one-inch pieces of cinnamon

Method

Mix the chicken with all the ingredients in a large microwave bowl

Refrigerate for 2 hours or more
When ready to cook, remove from the fridge
Add 1 cup of water and mix well

Cover the dish with a lid with holes or plastic or plastic wrap, leaving one side unsealed for venting

Microwave on high for 6 minutes.

Remove and mix well

Microwave again for 5 minutes more till done

Serve as a side dish with dhal and rice or Pepper Water and rice.

It could also be served as a starter or appetizer.

9. CHICKEN LIVER PEPPER FRY

Ingredients
½ kg chicken livers cut into pieces
2 large onions sliced finely
2 or 3 teaspoons ground black pepper / pepper powder
2 green chillies slit
Salt to taste
3 tablespoons oil

Method
Rinse the chicken livers

Mix the chicken livers with all the ingredients in a large microwave bowl

Keep aside for 30 to 45 minutes in the fridge

When ready to cook, remove from the
Add ½ cup of water

Cover the dish with a lid with holes or plastic wrap, leaving one side unsealed for venting

Microwave on high for 5 minutes.
Remove and mix well

Microwave again for 3 minutes more till done

Serve as a snack or side dish with bread or rice

10. CHICKEN JALFRAZIE

Ingredients
1 kg Boneless Chicken cut into cubes
1 teaspoon cumin seeds
3 dry red chillies broken into bits
2 teaspoons ginger garlic paste
2 tomatoes chopped
2 onions sliced finely
2 capsicums chopped into medium sized pieces
2 green chillies chopped
1 teaspoon spice powder or garam masala powder
1 teaspoon peppercorns
3 tablespoons oil
Salt to taste

Mix the chicken with all the ingredients in a large microwave bowl
Refrigerate for 2 hours or more
When ready to cook, remove from the fridge and bring to room temperature
Add ½ cup of water
Cover the dish with a lid with holes or plastic wrap, leaving one side unsealed for venting
Microwave on high for 8 minutes.
Remove and mix well
Microwave again for 5 minutes more till done
Serve as a side with pepper water and rice or chapattis, bread, dinner Rolls etc.

9. MICROWAVE MEAT DISHES

1. ANGLO-INDIAN MEAT BALL CURRY / BAD WORD CURRY

Ingredients: For the Curry

2 large onions chopped finely
1 sprig curry leaves
1 or 2 teaspoons chillie powder
1 teaspoon coriander powder
½ teaspoon turmeric powder
2 teaspoons ginger garlic paste
2 big tomatoes pureed
2 teaspoons coriander leaves chopped
½ cup coconut milk

1 teaspoon garam masala powder
Salt to taste
3 tablespoons oil

Ingredients for the Meat Balls
½ kg fine beef mince or lamb / mutton mince
½ teaspoon garam masala powder
½ teaspoon chillie powder
½ teaspoon turmeric powder
2 green chilies chopped
3 tablespoons coriander leaves chopped finely
Salt to taste

Method

First get the meat balls ready.
Mix the garam masala powder, chillie powder, turmeric powder, salt, chopped green chilies, and coriander leaves with the mince and form into small balls or koftas
Keep aside

Take a microwave safe dish and add the oil to it. Spread well on the base.

Mix all the curry ingredients together and transfer to the dish

Cover the dish with a lid with holes or plastic wrap, leaving one side unsealed for venting

Microwave on high for 3 minutes. Remove and mix

Place the meat balls carefully in the curry ingredients in the dish

Cover the dish with a lid with holes or plastic wrap, leaving one side unsealed for venting

Microwave on high for 8 minutes.
Remove and mix gently

Microwave again on medium heat for 8 minutes more till done with 4-minute rests

Serve with Yellow Coconut Rice or Steamed white Rice

2. SIMPLE BEEF CURRY

Ingredients
½ kg beef from the Round Portion
cut into small pieces
3 teaspoons chopped garlic
1 teaspoon chillie powder
3 onions sliced
Salt to taste
2 green chillies chopped
½ teaspoon turmeric powder
½ teaspoon ground black pepper/ pepper powder
2 tablespoons oil
2 tablespoons vinegar

Method
Mix the Beef with all the ingredients in a large microwave bowl
Refrigerate overnight

When ready to cook, remove from the fridge
Add ½ cup of water

Cover the dish with a lid with holes or plastic wrap, leaving one side unsealed for venting

Microwave on high for 8 minutes.
Remove and mix well

Microwave again for 6 minutes more till done with 3-minute rests

Serve as a side with rice or chapattis, bread, dinner Rolls etc.

3. ANGLO-INDIAN BEEF MINCE FRY

This is a quick and easy dish to cook when one has a packet of mince handy in the fridge but not too keen on making a Ball Curry. This simple and tasty dish could be eaten with Rice or Chapattis. Any meat mince such as beef, mutton, lamb, pork or even chicken mince could be used. Green Peas, chopped cabbage, carrot, cauliflower, fenugreek / methi / venthium greens etc., could be added to give the dish a twist.

Ingredients
½ kg Beef Mince / Ground Beef or Lamb Mince
1 big onion chopped finely
1 teaspoon chillie powder
½ teaspoon turmeric powder
1 teaspoon chopped garlic
1 teaspoon chopped ginger
2 green chilies chopped finely

2 tablespoons chopped coriander leaves
2 or 3 tablespoons oil
Salt to taste

Method

Mix the Beef Mince with all the ingredients in a large microwave bowl
Refrigerate for one hour or more. When ready to cook, remove from the fridge

Cover the dish with a lid with holes or plastic wrap, leaving one side unsealed for venting. Microwave on high for 5 minutes.

Remove and mix well to break up the minced beef / ground beef. Microwave again on medium heat for 6 minutes more till done with 3-minute rests.

Serve as a side with rice or chapattis, bread, dinner Rolls etc.

4. ANGLO-INDIAN BEEF PEPPER FRY

Another popular and frequently made dish in Anglo-Indian homes. You could substitute the Beef with mutton, lamb, pork etc.

Ingredients
½ kg tender Beef from the Round portion or loin cut into small pieces
3 teaspoons fresh ground black pepper
1 teaspoon chopped ginger
2 big onions sliced finely
3 tablespoons oil
3 large potatoes peeled and cut into quarters
Salt to taste

Method

Mix the Beef with all the ingredients in a large microwave bowl

Refrigerate for 2 hours or overnight.

When ready to cook, remove from the fridge and add ½ cup water

Cover the dish with a lid with holes or plastic wrap, leaving one side unsealed for venting.

Microwave on high for 10 minutes. Remove and mix well

Microwave again on medium heat for 6 minutes more till done with 3-minute rests.

Serve as a side with rice or chapattis, bread, dinner Rolls etc.

5. BEEF PEPPER STEAK

Ingredients

1kg Beef Undercut cut into thin steaks
3 or 4 teaspoons fresh ground black pepper powder
3 tablespoons oil
2 big onions sliced finely
2 big tomatoes chopped
Salt to taste

Method

Pat the steaks down gently with paper towels.
Then, season both sides with salt, pepper, (or whatever other spices you prefer)

Place the steak in a microwave safe dish along with the onions and tomatoes

Cover the dish with a lid with holes or plastic wrap, leaving one side unsealed for venting

Microwave for 5 minutes on High

Flip the steaks over and Microwave on high for minutes or more till done as per your choice

6. MUTTON CURRY / LAMB CURRY

Ingredients
½ kg mutton or lamb cut into medium pieces
3 tablespoons oil
2 large onions chopped finely
1 tablespoon ginger garlic paste
½ teaspoon turmeric powder
2 teaspoons chillie powder
1 teaspoon cumin powder
1 teaspoon coriander powder
2 tomatoes chopped
Salt to taste
2 tablespoons chopped coriander leaves
2 medium size potatoes peeled and cut into quarters

Method
Mix the Mutton or Lamb with all the ingredients in a large microwave bowl. Refrigerate for 2 or 3 hours or overnight

When ready to cook, remove from the fridge and add ½ cup water

Cover the dish with a lid with holes or plastic wrap, leaving one side unsealed for venting

Microwave on high for 6 minutes. Remove and mix well

Microwave again on medium heat for 6 minutes or more till done with 3-minute rests

Add 1 cup of warm water and mix in if more gravy is required. Microwave for 2 more minutes

Serve with rice or chapattis, bread, dinner Rolls etc.

7. MUTTON / LAMB MASALA CHOPS

Ingredients
½ kg good mutton / lamb chops
2 teaspoons ginger garlic paste
2 tablespoons vinegar
2 large onions sliced fine
2 or 3 green chilies sliced lengthwise
3 tablespoons oil
2 teaspoons chillie powder
1 teaspoon ground black pepper / pepper powder
Salt to taste
1 teaspoon cumin powder
1 teaspoon coriander powder

Method
Mix the Mutton or Lamb with all the ingredients in a large microwave bowl. Refrigerate for 2 or 3 hours or overnight

When ready to cook, remove from the fridge and add 1 cup water

Cover the dish with a lid with holes or plastic wrap, leaving one side unsealed for venting.

Microwave on high for 10 minutes. Remove and mix well

Microwave again on medium heat for 6 minutes or more or till done with 3-minute rests.

Serve with rice or chapattis, bread, dinner Rolls etc.

Note: You could use the same recipe for Beef or Veal Chops if desired.

8. MUTTON / LAMB STEW

Ingredients

¾ kg tender Mutton or lamb cut into medium size pieces
2 onions chopped finely
1 teaspoon chillie powder
1 teaspoon cumin Powder
1 tablespoon ginger garlic paste
3 tablespoons chopped coriander leaves
1 tablespoon chopped mint leaves
3 green chillies
4 cloves
8 black pepper corns

2 small pieces cinnamon
2 bay leaves
1 cup coconut milk or coconut cream
Salt to taste
3 tablespoons oil

Method

Mix the Mutton or Lamb with all the ingredients in a large microwave bowl.

Refrigerate for 2 or 3 hours or overnight

When ready to cook, remove from the fridge and add 1 cup water

Cover the dish with a lid with holes or plastic wrap, leaving one side unsealed for venting

Microwave on high for 10 minutes. Remove and mix well

Microwave again on medium heat for 6 minutes or more till done with 3-minute rests

Add 1 cup of warm water and mix in. Microwave for 2 more minutes

Serve with rice or chapattis, bread, dinner Rolls etc.

Note: You could substitute the Mutton or lamb with beef, veal, chicken, duck etc

9. RAILWAY MUTTON CURRY

Ingredients

½ kg tender lamb or mutton curry cut into medium size pieces (preferably boneless)
1 teaspoon whole peppercorns
2 big onions sliced finely
2 pieces cinnamon (about one inch in size)
2 or 3 cloves
2 dry red chilies broken into bits
2 teaspoons chillie powder (less spicy variety)
1 teaspoon cumin powder
2 teaspoons coriander powder
2 teaspoons ginger garlic paste
Salt to taste
3 or 4 tablespoons oil
3 potatoes peeled and cut into quarters

Method
Mix the Mutton or Lamb with all the ingredients in a large microwave bowl. Refrigerate for 2 or 3 hours or overnight. Remove from the fridge when ready to cook and add 1 cup water

Cover the dish with a lid with holes or plastic wrap, leaving one side unsealed for venting

Microwave on high for 10 minutes. Remove and mix well. Microwave again on medium heat for 6 minutes or more till done
Add ½ cup of tamarind juice and mix in.
Microwave for 2 more minutes

Serve with rice or chapattis, bread, dinner Rolls etc.

10. PEPPER LAMB / MUTTON SOFT RIB CHOPS

Ingredients
½ kg either Lamb or Mutton soft Spare Ribs
1teaspoon chopped ginger
1 teaspoon chopped garlic
2 tablespoons vinegar
2 large onions sliced fine
2 or 3 green chilies sliced lengthwise
3 tablespoons oil
2 teaspoons pepper powder
Salt to taste

Method
Mix the Ribs with all the ingredients in a large microwave bowl. Refrigerate overnight

When ready to cook, remove from the fridge and add 1 cup of water

Cover the dish with a lid with holes or plastic wrap, leaving one side unsealed for venting

Microwave on high for 8 minutes. Remove and mix well

Microwave again for 6 minutes or more till done with 3-minute rests

Garnish with onion rings.

10. MICROWAVE PORK DISHES

1. ANGLO-INDIAN PORK VINDALOO

Ingredients
½ kg pork loin cut into medium size pieces
2 teaspoons chillie powder
½ teaspoon turmeric powder
½ teaspoon mustard powder or paste
1 teaspoon cumin powder
2 tablespoons oil
Salt to taste

2 tablespoons ginger garlic paste
2 small sticks cinnamon
4 cloves
3 tablespoons vinegar

Method

Mix the Pork with all the ingredients in a large microwave bowl.

Refrigerate overnight

When ready to cook, remove from the fridge and add ½ of cup water

Cover the dish with a lid with holes or plastic wrap, leaving one side unsealed for venting

Microwave on high for 10 minutes. Remove and mix well

Microwave again on medium heat for 10 minutes more till done with 5-minute rests in between. Stir well

Leave aside with the lid on for 10 minutes to allow all the flavours to settle in.

Serve with rice or chapattis, bread, dinner Rolls etc. Pork Vindaloo goes really well with Coconut Rice

2. TANGY PORK CURRY
(Pork in a Tamarind Base)

Ingredients

½ kg pork loin with the fat and lard cut into medium pieces
2 big onions sliced finely
3 big tomatoes pureed or chopped finely
½ teaspoon cumin powder
1 teaspoon coriander powder
½ teaspoon turmeric powder
1 teaspoon garam masala powder
1 or 2 teaspoons chillie powder
2 teaspoons ginger garlic paste
2 tablespoons oil
Salt to taste

Method

Mix the pork with all the ingredients in a large microwave bowl. Refrigerate overnight

Remove from the fridge when ready to cook and add 1 cup water

Cover the dish with a lid with holes or plastic wrap, leaving one side unsealed for venting

Microwave on high for 10 minutes with 5 minute rests. Remove and mix well

Microwave again on medium heat for 6 minutes more till done with 3-minute rests

Add ½ cup tamarind juice extracted from a small ball of tamarind or ½ teaspoon tamarind concentrate and mix well.

Microwave for 2 minutes more.

Leave aside for 10 minutes before serving to allow the pork to absorb the Tamarind flavour

Serve with Rice, bread or any Indian bread

3. SPICY PORK CHOPS

Ingredients
½ kg good pork chops (rib chops)
2 teaspoons ginger garlic paste
2 tablespoons vinegar
2 large onions sliced finely
2 or 3 green chilies sliced lengthwise
3 tablespoons oil
1 teaspoon chillie powder
1 teaspoon all spice powder or garam masala
1 teaspoon ground black pepper/pepper powder
Salt to taste
3 tablespoons tomato sauce/ketchup

Method
Marinate the pork chops with all the above ingredients in a microwave safe dish for about 5 hours or overnight and leave in the fridge

Remove from the fridge when ready to cook and add ½ cup of water

Cover the dish with a lid with holes or plastic wrap, leaving one side unsealed for venting.

Microwave on high for 5 minutes. Remove and mix well

Microwave again on medium heat for 5 minutes. Remove and mix again.

Microwave for 4 minutes more.

Leave aside for 10 minutes before serving

Serve with Rice, bread or any Indian bread

4. ANGLO-INDIAN SPICY PORK FRY

Ingredients
½ kg Pork Belly or Loin cut into small pieces
3 whole red chillies broken into bits
½ teaspoon ground black pepper powder
½ teaspoon chillie powder
½ teaspoon pepper corns
3 cloves
2 small pieces of cinnamon
1 Bay leaf
 Salt to taste
2 tablespoons vinegar

Method
Marinate the pork with all the above ingredients in a microwave safe dish for about 3 to 4 hours

Add ½ cup of water

Cover the dish with a microwave safe lid with holes or plastic wrap, leaving one side unsealed for venting

Microwave on high for 5 minutes.
Remove and mix well

Microwave again for 5 minutes
Remove and mix again.

Microwave for 4 minutes more.

Leave aside for 10 minutes before serving

Serve with Rice, bread or any Indian bread

5. ANGLO-INDIAN PORK CURRY

Ingredients
½ kg pork (belly portion) cut into small pieces
2 onions sliced finely
1 or 2 teaspoons chillie powder
1 teaspoon coriander powder
½ teaspoon turmeric powder
2 tablespoons oil
Salt to taste
1 tablespoon ginger garlic paste
2 tomatoes chopped finely
2 green chillies
2 tablespoons vinegar

Method
Marinate the pork with all the above ingredients
in a microwave safe dish for about 3 to 4 hours.

Refrigerate till ready to cook. Add ½ cup of water

Cover the dish with a lid with holes or plastic
wrap, leaving one side unsealed for venting
Microwave on high for 5 minutes.

Remove and mix well

Microwave again for 5 minutes
Remove and mix again.

Microwave for 4 minutes more.

Leave aside for 10 minutes before serving

Serve with Rice, bread or any Indian bread

6. DEVILLED PORK CHOPS

Ingredients
1 kg Pork Chops (Rib chops)
4 green chilies ground to a paste
1 teaspoon mustard powder
2 tablespoons Worcestershire / Soya sauce
2 teaspoon chillie powder
1 teaspoon coriander powder
Salt to taste
2 tablespoons oil
1 teaspoon peppercorns
3 onions sliced finely
2 tablespoons vinegar
2 teaspoons Worcestershire sauce
3 Potatoes boiled and cut into halves

Method

Marinate the pork with all the above ingredients
in a microwave safe dish for about 3 to 4 hours

Add ½ cup of water before cooking

Cover the dish with a microwave safe lid with holes or plastic wrap, leaving one side unsealed for venting

Microwave on high for 5 minutes. Remove and mix well

Microwave again for 5 minutes
Remove and mix again.

Microwave for 4 minutes more.

Leave aside for 10 minutes before serving

Serve with Rice, bread or any Indian bread

7. PORK PEPPER SHORT RIBS

Ingredients

1 kg Pork Short Ribs
1 teaspoon Coriander Powder
2 teaspoons ground black pepper
2 teaspoons finely chopped garlic
2 tablespoons oil
Salt to taste
½ teaspoon chillie powder or paprika
2 tablespoons vinegar
3 onions finely chopped

Marinate the pork with all the above ingredients in a microwave safe dish for about 3 to 4 hours

Add ½ cup of water and shake the dish

Cover the dish with a microwave safe lid with holes or plastic wrap, leaving one side unsealed for venting

Microwave on high for 5 minutes. Remove and mix well

Microwave again for 5 minutes
Remove and mix again.

Microwave for 4 minutes more.

Leave aside for 10 minutes before serving

Serve with rice or Bread. This could also be served as a snack or a starter.

8. PORK PEPPER FRY

Ingredients
1 kg tender pork (belly portion) cut into cubes
2 green chillies sliced
3 onions sliced finely
2 teaspoons chopped garlic
1 teaspoon chopped ginger
3 or 4 teaspoons ground black pepper
8 or 10 curry leaves (optional)
Salt to taste

Marinate the pork with all the above ingredients in a microwave safe dish for about 3 to 4 hours

Add ½ cup of water

Cover the dish with a microwave safe lid with holes or plastic wrap, leaving one side unsealed for venting

Microwave on high for 5 minutes. Remove and mix well

Microwave again for 5 minutes
Remove and mix again.

Microwave for 3 minutes more.

Leave aside for 10 minutes before serving

Serve as a side dish with Rice or bread

9. SPICY PORK MINCE

Ingredients

½ kg Pork Mince/Ground Pork
1 big onion chopped finely
1 teaspoon chillie powder
½ teaspoon turmeric powder
1 teaspoon chopped garlic
1 teaspoon chopped ginger
2 green chilies chopped finely
2 tablespoons chopped coriander leaves
2 or 3 tablespoons oil
Salt to taste

Method

Mix the Pork Mince with all the ingredients in a large microwave bowl.

Refrigerate for one hour or more.

When ready to cook, remove from the fridge.

Cover the dish with a lid with holes or plastic wrap, leaving one side unsealed for venting

Microwave on high for 5 minutes. Remove and mix well to break up the minced pork/ ground pork

Add a little water if some gravy is required.

Microwave again for 4 minutes more till done with 2-minute rests.

Serve as a side with rice or chapattis, bread, dinner Rolls etc.

10. PORK IN TOMATO GRAVY

Ingredients

½ kg Pork Belly cut into small pieces
2 onions sliced finely
2 teaspoons chillie powder
1 teaspoon cumin powder
1 teaspoon coriander powder
½ teaspoon turmeric powder
2 teaspoons ginger garlic paste
2 large tomatoes pureed
2 tablespoons oil
Salt to taste

Method

Marinate the pork with all the above ingredients in a microwave safe dish for about 3 to 4 hours

Cover the dish with a microwave safe lid with holes or plastic wrap, leaving one side unsealed for venting

Microwave on high for 5 minutes.
Remove and mix well

Microwave again on for 5 minutes
Remove and mix again.

Microwave for 4 minutes with 2-minute rests.

Check if the pork is cooked or microwave again for 3 more minutes.

Leave aside for 10 minutes before serving

Serve with Rice, bread or any Indian bread

11. MICROWAVE FISH & SEAFOOD DISHES

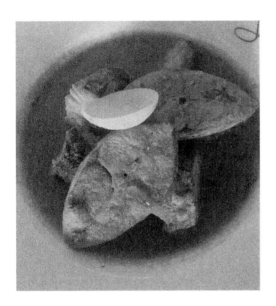

1. TANGY FISH CURRY (Fish cooked in a Tamarind Base)

Ingredients
½ kg of any fleshy fish cut into slices
2 green chillies sliced lengthwise
1 teaspoon coriander powder
½ teaspoon turmeric powder
2 teaspoons chillie powder
1 teaspoon ginger garlic paste

½ cup tamarind water extracted from a lime sized ball
Salt to taste
2 tablespoons Oil

Method

Marinate the fish with the chilli powder, coriander powder, turmeric powder, ginger garlic paste, tamarind water, turmeric, green chillies and salt. Leave aside for 1hour.

Take a large flat microwave dish and add the oil. Spread all over the bottom

Place the fish carefully in the dish

Cover the dish with a microwave safe lid with holes or plastic wrap, leaving one side unsealed for venting.

Microwave on high for 3 minutes.
Remove and turn the fish over

Microwave again on medium heat for 6 minutes
Remove and shake the dish to move the fish without breaking

Microwave for 3 minutes more on medium heat

Garnish with coriander and serve with Rice

2. SARDINES IN TOMATO GRAVY

Ingredients
½ kg Sardines or any other fish of your choice
2 onions sliced finely
2 tomatoes pureed or chopped finely
1 teaspoons ginger garlic paste
1 or 2 teaspoons chillie powder
1 teaspoon coriander powder
1 teaspoon cumin powder
¼ teaspoon turmeric powder
Salt to taste
2 tablespoons oil

Wash the sardines clean and keep aside.

Make a paste of the chillie powder, coriander powder, turmeric powder, cumin powder, salt and ginger garlic paste with a little water

Marinate the sardines with this paste. Leave aside for 1hour.

Take a large flat microwave dish and add the oil. Spread the sliced onions and chopped tomatoes or tomato puree all over the bottom of the dish Microwave on high for 3 minutes

Remove from the microwave and place the sardines carefully in the dish over this layer

Cover the dish with a microwave safe lid with holes or plastic wrap, leaving one side unsealed for venting

Microwave on high for 5 minutes. Remove and turn the sardines over

Microwave again on medium heat for 5 minutes Remove and shake the dish to move the fish without breaking

Leave aside for 10 minutes (Covered) before serving

Serve with Rice or Any Indian Bread

3. FISH MOLEY (FISH STEW)

Ingredients

½ kg Seer Fish /Spanish Blue Mackerel / King Fish or any other good fleshy fish of your choice sliced thickly
2 big onions sliced finely
4 green chilies sliced lengthwise
1 teaspoon chopped ginger
1 teaspoon chopped garlic
1 teaspoon crushed black pepper powder
1 teaspoon turmeric powder
1 teaspoon coriander powder
4 tablespoons oil
Salt to taste
1 tablespoon lime / lemon juice
1 cup thick coconut milk
3 tablespoons oil
1 medium size tomato chopped into 8 pieces
8 to 10 curry leaves

Method

Wash the fish well and rub all over with the turmeric powder, coriander powder, pepper powder, lime juice and a little salt. Leave aside for 1hour.

Take a large flat microwave dish and add the oil. Spread the curry leaves, sliced onions, chopped garlic, chopped ginger and the green chillies all over the bottom

Microwave on high for 2 minutes. Then remove the dish

Place the fish carefully in the dish
Cover the dish with a microwave safe lid with holes or plastic wrap, leaving one side unsealed for venting
Microwave on high (900 W) for 6 minutes.

Remove and turn the fish over
Microwave again on high heat for 5 minutes

Remove and add the coconut milk and chopped tomatoes

Shake the dish to move the fish without breaking and for the coconut milk to cover the fish
Microwave for 2 minutes more on high heat

Serve with Rice or Any Indian Bread

4. FISH CURRY IN COCONUT MILK

Ingredients
½ kg of any fleshy fish such as Sole, Pomfret,
Seer, etc., cut into slices or chunks
1 teaspoon chillie powder
2 teaspoons coriander powder
½ teaspoon cumin powder
½ teaspoon turmeric powder
2 green chillies slit lengthwise
1 teaspoon ginger garlic paste
1 cup coconut milk or coconut cream
Salt to taste

Method
Marinate the fish with the chilli powder,
coriander powder, cumin powder, turmeric
powder, ginger garlic paste, green chillies and
salt. Leave aside for 1 hour.

Take a large flat microwave dish and add the oil.
Spread the oil all over the bottom. Place the fish
carefully in the dish

Cover the dish with a microwave safe lid with
holes or plastic wrap, leaving one side unsealed
for venting. Microwave on high for 5 minutes.

Remove and turn the fish over. Microwave again
on high heat for 5 minutes

Remove the dish and pour the coconut milk over
it. Shake the dish a little. Microwave on high for
3 more minutes.
Garnish with coriander and serve with Rice or
Chapattis or Bread

5. FISH IN MUSTARD GRAVY

Ingredients
½ kg good fleshy fish such as Trout, Salmon, king fish etc
3 tablespoons mustard oil or any other cooking oil
1 tablespoon mustard seeds
3 green chillies
1 teaspoon coriander powder
¼ teaspoon turmeric powder
Salt to taste

Method

Make a paste of the mustard, chillies, coriander powder and turmeric powder with a little water.
Marinate the fish with the above mixture
Leave aside for 1hour.

Take a large flat microwave dish and add the oil. Spread all over the bottom. Place the fish carefully in the dish

Cover the dish with a microwave safe lid with holes or plastic wrap, leaving one side unsealed for venting. Microwave on high for 3 minutes.

Remove and turn the fish over. Microwave again on high for 6 minutes with 3-minute rests

Remove and shake the dish to move the fish without breaking. Microwave for 3 minutes more on medium heat. Serve with Rice

6. SIMPLE BAKED WHOLE FISH

Ingredients
1 whole fish such as pomfret, whitefish, trout, salmon, or halibut
Salt and Pepper to taste
Any other seasoning of your choice such as chillie powder, Rosemary, Tarragon, Oregano, Paprika etc
2 tablespoons butter
lemon wedges, for garnish

Method
Sprinkle the fish lightly with salt and pepper and any other seasoning of your choice on all sides. Refrigerate for about ½ hour

Place in a suitable flat microwave dish. Dot with the butter all over
Cover the dish with a microwave safe lid with holes or plastic wrap, leaving one side unsealed for venting. Microwave on high for 8 to 9 minutes. Let it stand covered for 5 minutes.

Serve warm, garnished with lemon wedges.

7. GREEN MASALA FISH

Ingredients
½ kg good fleshy fish cut into thick slices
1 teaspoon ginger garlic paste
½ cup chopped coriander leaves
1 teaspoon cumin powder
3 green chillies

¼ teaspoon turmeric powder
Salt to taste
2 tablespoons oil

Grind the green chillies, coriander leaves, cumin powder, ginger garlic paste, salt and turmeric powder together with a little water.

Marinate the fish slices with this paste and keep aside for half an hour.

Method

Take a large flat microwave dish and add the oil. Place the marinated fish carefully in the dish

Cover the dish with a microwave safe lid with holes or plastic wrap, leaving one side unsealed for venting. Microwave on high for 5 minutes.

Remove and turn the fish over. Microwave again for 5 minutes

Remove and shake the dish to move the fish without breaking

Leave covered for 10 minutes before serving

Garnish with coriander leaves and serve with Rice or Any Indian Bread

8. ANGLO-INDIAN PRAWN CURRY

Ingredients
300 grams Prawns (cleaned and deveined)
1 teaspoon chillie powder
1 teaspoon coriander powder
½ teaspoon cumin powder
½ teaspoon turmeric powder
1 teaspoon ginger garlic paste
2 tablespoons tomato puree or tomato paste
Salt to taste
2 tablespoons salt

Method

Marinate the prawns with the chilli powder, coriander powder, cumin powder, turmeric powder, ginger garlic paste, tomato paste / puree, oil and salt. Leave aside for 1 hour.

Transfer to a microwave dish

Cover the dish with a microwave safe lid with holes or plastic wrap, leaving one side unsealed for venting. Microwave on high for 5 minutes

Remove and mix. Microwave again on high heat for 3 minutes

Remove from the microwave and leave it covered for 5 minutes before serving

Garnish with coriander leaves and serve with Rice or Chapattis or Bread

9. PRAWN VINDALOO

Ingredients
½ kg fresh Shrimps or Prawns shelled and deveined
2 medium sized onions chopped
2 teaspoons chillie powder
2 teaspoons cumin powder
½ teaspoon pepper powder
2 teaspoons ginger garlic paste
3 tablespoons vinegar
Salt to taste
2 potatoes peeled and cut into quarters
3 tablespoons oil

Method
Marinate the prawns with all the above
ingredients for around 1 or 2 hours

Transfer to a large flat microwave dish
Cover the dish with a microwave safe lid with
holes or plastic wrap, leaving one side unsealed
for venting

Microwave on high (900 W) for 5 minutes.
Remove and mix well

Microwave again on high heat for 3 minutes

Leave covered for 5 minutes before serving

Serve with Rice or Any Indian Bread

10. SPICY PRAWN FRY

Ingredients
½ kg medium sized prawns cleaned and deveined
A few curry leaves
2 sliced onions
1 tablespoon ginger garlic paste
2 teaspoons chillie powder
1 teaspoon turmeric powder
1 teaspoon cumin powder
1 teaspoon garam masala powder
Juice of one lime
Salt to taste
4 tablespoons oil

Marinate the prawns with the chillie powder, turmeric powder, cumin powder, garam masala powder, lime juice and salt. Leave aside for 1hour.
Take a large flat microwave dish and add the oil. Spread the curry leaves, sliced onions, chopped garlic, chopped ginger and the green chillies over the bottom. Microwave on high for 2 minutes.
Remove the dish. Transfer the marinated prawns to the dish and spread evenly. Cover the dish with a microwave safe lid with holes or plastic wrap, leaving one side unsealed for venting
Microwave on high for 6 minutes. Remove and give it a mix
Microwave again on high heat for 3 minutes
Leave aside with the cover on for 5 minutes before serving. Garnish with chopped coriander.
Serve as a side dish or as a snack or starter

12. MICROWAVE EGG DISHES

1. SIMPLE EGG CURRY

Ingredients
6 hardboiled eggs cut in halves
2 small onions sliced finely
2 tomatoes pureed
1 teaspoon chillie powder
1 teaspoon coriander powder
½ teaspoon turmeric powder
2 tablespoons chopped coriander leaves
1 teaspoon ginger garlic paste
 Salt to taste
2 tablespoons oil

Method

Mix the chillie powder, turmeric powder, coriander powder, ginger garlic paste, salt and tomato puree to a smooth paste. Add ½ cup of water to it and mix well

Take a Microwave safe dish and add the oil and the onions.

Cover the dish with a lid with holes or plastic wrap, leaving one side unsealed for venting

Microwave on high for 2 minutes to allow the onions to cook a little. Remove and add the tomato spice paste

Cover the dish again and Microwave on high heat for 4 minutes

Add 1 cup of warm water and mix in if more gravy is required

Add the boiled egg halves and spoon the gravy over the eggs

Microwave for 1 more minute

Remove and garnish with chopped coriander leaves

Serve with rice or chapattis, etc

2. EGG VINDALOO

Ingredients
6   Hardboiled eggs shelled
2 onions chopped
2 teaspoons chilli powder
½ teaspoon turmeric powder
2 teaspoons ginger garlic paste
1 teaspoon cumin powder
½ cup tomato puree or tomato paste
2 pieces cinnamon
2 table spoons vinegar
1 teaspoon sugar
Salt to taste
3 tablespoons oil

Method

Mix the chilli powder, turmeric powder, cumin powder, ginger garlic paste, salt, sugar, cinnamon and tomato puree to a smooth paste.

Take a Microwave safe dish and add the oil and the onions. Cover the dish with a lid with holes or plastic wrap, leaving one side unsealed for venting

Microwave on high for 2 minutes to allow the onions to cook a little

Remove and add the tomato spice paste

Cover the dish again and Microwave on high heat for 4 minutes

Add 1 cup of warm water and mix in if more gravy is required

Add the boiled eggs and spoon the gravy over the eggs. Microwave for 1 more minute

Serve with rice or bread, etc.

3. EGG AND BRINJAL (AUBERGINE) CURRY

Ingredients
6 hardboiled eggs, peeled and halved
250 grams round or long Brinjals (Aubergines) cut into medium size pieces
2 tablespoons vinegar
Salt to taste
2 onions chopped finely
1 teaspoon finely chopped garlic
1 teaspoon finely chopped ginger
2 tablespoons Oil
¼ teaspoon turmeric powder
1 teaspoon cumin powder
2 teaspoon chillie powder
1 teaspoon coriander powder
1 small piece of cinnamon
3 cloves
2 tablespoons tomato paste or juice
2 tablespoons chopped coriander leaves

Method

Mix the chilli powder, turmeric powder, cumin powder, coriander powder, salt and tomato puree to a smooth paste. Add ½ a cup of water to it and mix well

Marinate the Brinjals with this mixture and leave aside

Take a Microwave safe dish and add the oil, onions, garlic, ginger, cinnamon and cloves

Cover the dish with a lid with holes or plastic wrap, leaving one side unsealed for venting

Microwave on high for 2 minutes to allow the onions to cook a little. Remove and add the marinated brinjals

Cover the dish again and Microwave on high heat for 6 minutes. Add 1 cup of warm water and mix in if more gravy is required

Add the boiled eggs and spoon the gravy over the eggs. Microwave for 1 more minute

Serve with rice or bread, etc.

4. BOILED EGGS AND CAULIFLOWER CURRY

Ingredients

6 or 8 hardboiled eggs, shelled and halved
2 onions sliced
1 cup cauliflower florets
1 teaspoon ginger garlic paste
3 green chilies
3 tablespoons coriander leaves
1 teaspoon cumin powder

1 teaspoon chilli powder
½ teaspoon turmeric powder
Salt to taste
3 tablespoons oil

Method

Mix the chilli powder, turmeric powder, cumin powder, ginger garlic paste and salt to a smooth with ½ a cup of water

Mix the cauliflower florets with this mixture

Take a Microwave safe dish and add the oil, onions and green chillies

Cover the dish with a lid with holes or plastic wrap, leaving one side unsealed for venting

Microwave on high for 2 minutes to allow the onions to cook a little

Remove and add the cauliflower mixture

Cover the dish again and Microwave on high heat for 6 minutes

Add 1 cup of warm water and mix in if more gravy is required. Add the boiled eggs and spoon the gravy over the eggs

Microwave for 1 more minute. Garnish with coriander leaves

Serve with rice or roti, chapattis, etc

5. EGG MOILEE

Ingredients
6 hardboiled eggs shelled and halved
2 small onions sliced finely
4 green chilies sliced lengthwise
1 teaspoon chopped ginger
1 teaspoon chopped garlic
1 teaspoon crushed black pepper powder
1 teaspoon turmeric powder
1 teaspoon coriander powder
4 tablespoons oil
Salt to taste
1 tablespoon lime / lemon juice
1 cup thick coconut milk
3 tablespoons oil
1 medium size tomato chopped into 8 pieces
8 to 10 curry leaves

Method

Mix the turmeric powder, coriander powder, pepper powder, lime juice and salt with ½ cup of water

Take a large flat microwave dish and add the oil. Spread the curry leaves, sliced onions, chopped garlic, chopped ginger and the green chillies all over the bottom

Microwave on high for 2 minutes. Then remove the dish

Add the paste to the dish

Cover the dish with a microwave safe lid with holes or plastic wrap, leaving one side unsealed for venting

Microwave on high for 3 minutes

Remove and mix in the coconut milk and chopped tomatoes

Place the egg halves on top and lightly spoon the gravy on top

Microwave covered on high for 2 more minutes

Serve with steamed rice or bread

6. EGGS AND HAM BAKE

Ingredients
4 Eggs
6 slices of Ham
2 small tomatoes sliced
½ cup Shredded Mozzarella Cheese
2 teaspoons butter
Salt, Pepper and Mixed Herbs Seasoning to taste
Parsley or Coriander leaves to garnish

Method

Take a microwave safe dish and grease it with the butter

Layer the slices of Ham in such a way that it covers the bottom and up the sides of the dish, pressing well into the corners

Sprinkle some cheese over the ham

Now crack the eggs onto the ham and cheese

Randomly scatter the slices of tomato

Season with salt, pepper and mixed herb seasoning

Cover with a lid or plate. Microwave on high for 3 minutes

If you need the yolks to be little harder, microwave for one more minute

Garnish with chopped parsley or coriander

Serve with warm toasted bread and butter

7. EGG QUICHE

Ingredients
6 Eggs
½ cup milk
6 slices of ham – cut into small pieces
3 slices of bread – cut into small cubes
3 tablespoons shredded mozzarella cheese
1 teaspoon fresh or dried chopped parsley
1 small onion chopped
1 teaspoon Djon mustard
Salt and pepper to season

Method
Beat egg and milk together with a fork adding salt and pepper to taste.

Mix in the ham, bread, cheese, mustard and onion

Transfer to a Microwave safe dish. Sprinkle the parsley on top

Microwave on high for 2 minutes.

Garnish with chives or parsley if desired

8. BAKED EGGS WITH HAM, SPINACH AND ONIONS

Ingredients
3 Eggs
½ cup chopped spinach either fresh or frozen
3 tablespoons grated cheese
1 small onion sliced
1 small tomato chopped
2 teaspoons butter
Salt, Pepper and any other seasoning to taste

Method
Grease a microwave safe dish with the butter
Layer the ham, spinach, onion, tomatoes in the dish

Break the eggs on this layer and break the yolks so that the yolks spread a little. Sprinkle the grated cheese on top

Season with salt, pepper and any other seasoning of your choice

Cover with a plate or a microwave safe lid. Microwave on high for 2 minutes. Serve with toast and any sauce

9. EGG, PEPPERONI AND MUSHROOM BAKE

Ingredients
6 Eggs beaten
½ cup pepperoni thinly sliced
2 tablespoons butter
1 small onion sliced finely
1 green chillie chopped
3 or 4 mushrooms sliced
1 small tomato sliced
Salt and pepper to taste

Method

Take a microwave dish and add the butter and onions. Microwave on high for 2 minutes

Remove and add the mushrooms and green chillies. Microwave on high for 1 minute and 30 seconds

Remove and spread the pepperoni then pour the beaten eggs over it

Season with salt, pepper and any other seasoning of your choice

Cover with a plate or lid and microwave on high for 2 minutes

Wait for it to cool a bit, then cut into portions

Serve with toasted garlic bread and potato wafers

10. EGG, BREAD AND HAM COBBLER

Ingredients
2 slices white or whole meal bread
2 tablespoons butter or oil
4 slices of ham cut into halves
6 Eggs
½ cup milk
½ cup grated cheese
Salt and pepper to taste

Method
Take a microwave safe dish and spread some butter or oil on the bottom
Butter the bread and cut each sliced into quarters. Arrange the bread at the bottom of the dish
Spread the ham over the bread
Beat the eggs well and add the milk, salt and pepper and any other seasoning of your choice
Pour this milk mixture over the bread and ham and wait for the bread to get completely soaked. (Press down the bread with a spoon)
Cover with a plate or a microwave safe lid
Microwave on high for 4 minutes
Remove the dish from the oven and sprinkle the grated cheese on top
Microwave again on high for 1 minute
Leave the dish covered for 2 minutes before serving
Serve with a salad and potato wafers

13. MICROWAVE VEGETABLE CURRIES AND SIDE DISHES

1. MIXED VEGETABLE CURRY

Ingredients
2 cups of chopped mixed vegetables such as carrots, potato, cauliflower etc (chopped into bite size pieces). Add some peas also if desired
2 small onions sliced very finely
1 teaspoon chillie powder,
½ teaspoon turmeric powder
1 teaspoon ginger garlic paste
1 teaspoon cumin powder
½ teaspoon fennel powder

2 tomatoes chopped
1 tablespoon vinegar
Salt to taste,
3 tablespoons oil

Method
Mix all the ingredients together in a microwave safe dish
Cover the dish with a microwave safe lid with holes or plastic wrap, leaving one side unsealed for venting
Microwave on high for 3 minutes
Take out and stir and microwave for 3 more minutes
Add 1 cup of water and mix gently
Check if the vegetables are cooked or microwave for 2 more minutes
Leave aside to cool a bit before serving
Serve with Rice or any Indian Bread

2. SIMPLE POTATO CURRY

Ingredients
3 potatoes peeled and cut into medium size pieces
1 teaspoon chillie powder
1 teaspoon cumin powder,
1 teaspoon garlic and ginger paste
1 teaspoon coriander powder,
½ teaspoon turmeric powder
3 tablespoons tomato puree or paste
2 tablespoons oil,
Salt to taste

Mix the potatoes with all the above ingredients and half cup of water in a microwave safe dish

Cover the dish with a microwave safe lid with holes or plastic wrap, leaving one side unsealed for venting
Microwave on high (900 W) for 3 minutes
Take out and stir and microwave for 3 more minutes
Add some more water if more gravy is desired and mix gently
Check if the potatoes are cooked or microwave for 2 more minutes
Leave aside to cool a bit before serving
Serve with Rice or any Indian Bread

3. POTATO, PEAS AND CAULIFLOWER CURRY

Ingredients
1 cup cauliflower florets
2 potatoes peeled and cut into medium size pieces
½ cup green peas either fresh or frozen
1onion chopped
1 tablespoon chopped coriander leaves
1 tomato chopped,
3 tablespoons ground coconut
2 teaspoons chillie powder
½ teaspoon turmeric
½ teaspoon cumin powder
1 teaspoon coriander powder
2 small pieces cinnamon
1 bay leaf
Salt to taste
2 tablespoons oil

Mix the chilli powder, turmeric powder, cumin powder, coriander powder and salt to a smooth mixture with ½ a cup of water

Marinate the cauliflower florets, potatoes and peas with this mixture

Take a Microwave safe dish and add the oil, onions, cinnamon and bay leaf

Cover the dish with a lid with holes or plastic wrap, leaving one side unsealed for venting

Microwave on high for 2 minutes to allow the onions to cook a little

Remove and add the marinated vegetables, tomatoes and coconut

Cover the dish again and Microwave on high heat for 4 minutes

Take out and stir

Microwave on high for 3 more minutes

Add some more water if more gravy is desired and mix gently

Microwave for 3 more minutes

Leave aside to cool a bit before serving

Serve with Rice or any Indian Bread

4. BRINJAL (EGGPLANT) AND POTATO VINDALOO

Ingredients

½ kg small round brinjals / eggplant cut into halves

2 potatoes peeled and cut into quarters

2 onions sliced finely

1 teaspoon chillie powder

½ teaspoon turmeric powder

1 teaspoon cumin powder

1 teaspoon ginger garlic paste

½ cup tomato puree
2 pieces cinnamon
2 table spoons vinegar
1teaspoon sugar
Salt to taste
3 tablespoons oil

Method
Mix the chilli powder, turmeric powder, cumin powder, salt, sugar, ginger garlic paste, vinegar and tomato puree to a smooth paste.

Marinate the Brinjals and potatoes with this paste and leave aside

Take a Microwave safe dish and add the oil, onions and cinnamon

Cover the dish with a lid with holes or plastic wrap, leaving one side unsealed for venting
Microwave on high for 2 minutes to allow the onions to cook a little

Remove and add the marinated Brinjals and Potatoes. Cover the dish again and Microwave on high heat for 4 minutes

Add 1/2 cup of warm water and mix in (Add more water if more gravy is required)
Microwave for 2 more minutes
Serve with rice or bread, etc.

5. SPINACH AND POTATO SIDE DISH

Ingredients
3 medium size potatoes peeled and cut into small
size pieces
1 cup chopped spinach
2 green chillies chopped finely
6 or 8 curry leaves
½ teaspoon cumin powder
1 teaspoon chillie powder
Salt to taste
½ teaspoon turmeric powder
2 tablespoons oil

Method
Mix the potatoes with the chilli powder, turmeric
powder, cumin powder, and salt

Take a Microwave safe dish and add the oil, green
chillies and curry leaves
Cover the dish with a lid with holes or plastic
wrap, leaving one side unsealed for venting

Microwave on high for 1 minute
Remove and add the marinated Potatoes

Cover the dish again and Microwave on high heat
for 5 minutes

Add the chopped spinach and mix in

Microwave for 2 more minutes

Serve with rice, rotis, chapattis, etc.

6. MIXED VEGETABLE STEW

Ingredients
2 cups of chopped mixed vegetables such as carrot, potato, cauliflower, knolkol etc. (Cut into bite size pieces)
2 onions sliced
3 green chillies slit lengthwise
1 teaspoon chopped garlic
1 teaspoon chopped ginger,
1 teaspoon whole pepper corns
2 cloves
2 pieces cinnamon
1 cup thick coconut milk
Salt to taste
2 tablespoons oil

Method
Take a Microwave safe dish and add the oil, onions, green chillies, ginger, garlic, pepper corns and whole spices
Cover the dish with a lid with holes (or plastic wrap, leaving one side unsealed for venting)
Microwave on high for 2 minutes the onions turn transparent
Remove and add the vegetables, salt and ½ cup of water.
Cover the dish again and Microwave on high heat for 3 minutes. Remove and stir. Microwave for 3 more minutes
Add the coconut milk and mix in
Microwave for 2 more minutes
Serve with rice, bread, hoppers, rotis, chapattis, etc.

7. SPICY GLAZED CARROTS

Ingredients
300 grams baby carrots
2 tablespoons butter
½ teaspoon sugar
1 teaspoon chillie powder
3 green chillies slit lengthwise
1 teaspoon lime juice
1 tablespoon chopped coriander leaves,
Salt to taste

Method
Mix the carrots with the chilli powder, salt, sugar, green chillies and lime juice
Transfer all to a microwave safe dish with 2 tablespoons water
Cover the dish with a lid with holes (or plastic wrap, leaving one side unsealed for venting)
Microwave on high for 3 minutes
Remove and check if the carrots are done.
If you like them softer and not so crunchy, microwave for 1 minute more
Add the butter and season with ground pepper and any other seasoning as desired
Garnish with coriander leaves.
Serve as a side dish with steamed rice

8. BEANS AND CARROT FOOGATH

Ingredients
½ kg string beans chopped finely
3 tender carrots chopped into small pieces
½ cup grated coconut
1 teaspoon chopped ginger
3 red chilies broken into bits

¼ teaspoon mustard seeds
A few curry leaves
Salt to taste
2 tablespoons oil

Method
Take a Microwave safe dish and add the oil, mustard seeds, chillies, curry leaves and ginger
Cover the dish with a lid with holes (or plastic wrap, leaving one side unsealed for venting)
Microwave on high for 1 minute till the mustard seeds pop. Remove, and add the chopped beans and carrots, salt and ½ cup of water
Cover the dish again and Microwave on high heat for 3 minutes. Remove and stir.
Microwave for 3 more minutes
Add the grated coconut and mix in
Serve as a side dish with rice and curry

9. CAULIFLOWER FOOGATH

Ingredients
1 small cauliflower chopped into very small florets or bits
2 or 3 dry red chilies broken into bits
1 onion sliced finely
2 pods of garlic chopped
¼ teaspoon mustard seeds
1 sprig curry leaves
½ cup grated coconut (optional)
2 tablespoons oil
Salt to taste

Method
Take a Microwave safe dish and add the oil, onions, mustard seeds, curry leaves, chillies and garlic

Cover the dish with a lid with holes (or plastic wrap, leaving one side unsealed for venting)
Microwave on high for 2 minutes till the onions soften
Remove and add the chopped cauliflower, salt and ½ cup of water. Cover the dish again and Microwave on high heat for 3 minutes
Remove and stir. Microwave for 3 more minutes
Add the grated coconut and mix in
Serve as a side dish with rice and curry

10. CABBAGE FOOGATH

Ingredients
1 small cabbage chopped finely
3 tablespoons grated coconut (optional)
1 teaspoon chopped ginger
2 green chillies chopped or 2 dry red chillies broken
¼ teaspoon mustard seeds
A few curry leaves
Salt to taste
2 tablespoons oil

Method
Take a Microwave safe dish and add the oil, mustard seeds, chillies, curry leaves and ginger

Cover the dish with a lid with holes (or plastic wrap, leaving one side unsealed for venting)

Microwave on high for 1 minute till the mustard seeds pop. Remove and add the chopped cabbage and 2 tablespoons of water

Cover the dish again and Microwave on high heat for 3 minutes. Remove and stir.

Microwave for 3 more minutes. Add the grated coconut and mix in

Serve as a side dish with rice and curry

14. MICROWAVE RICE DISHES

1. PLAIN WHITE STEAMED RICE

Ingredients
1 cup raw rice of your choice
1.5 cups water
A pinch of salt

Wash the rice and soak in 2 cups of water and a pinch of salt for 5 minutes in a large microwave safe bowl (rice expands while cooking so choose a suitable bowl that is large enough)
Microwave on high heat for 10 minutes with 5-minute rests

At this point, small steam holes will appear in the rice and most of the water would be absorbed

Now cover the dish with a lid with holes (or plastic wrap, leaving one side unsealed for venting)

Microwave on high for 5 more minutes

Remove the dish and leave it covered for 10 minutes. Do not stir the rice

Fluff with a fork before serving with any curry or side dish

2. SAFFRON COCONUT RICE / YELLOW RICE

Ingredients

1 pack of coconut milk (250 ml) diluted with water to get 4 cups of milk

2 cups of Raw Rice or Basmati Rice (any long-grained rice of your choice)

½ teaspoon turmeric powder or a few strands of saffron

Salt to taste

4 tablespoons butter or ghee

3 cloves, 3 cardamoms, 3 small sticks of cinnamon

Wash the rice and soak with all the above ingredients in a large microwave safe dish

Microwave on high heat for 10 minutes with 5-minute rests each time

At this point, small steam holes will appear in the rice and most of the liquid would be absorbed

Now cover the dish with a lid with holes (or plastic wrap, leaving one side unsealed for venting)

Microwave on high for 5 more minutes

Remove the dish and leave it covered for 10 minutes. Do not stir the rice
Fluff with a fork before serving
Coconut Rice is best eaten with Ball Curry or Chicken curry and Devil Chutney.

3. CHICKEN PISH-PASH RICE OR SMASHED RICE

Ingredients
1 cup raw rice
250 grams boneless chicken cut into tiny pieces
1 teaspoon whole pepper corns
1 small piece of cinnamon
½ teaspoon chopped ginger
Salt to taste
1tablespoon butter or ghee
A few mint leaves or ½ teaspoon dry mint (optional)

Method
Wash the rice and soak in 3 cups of water and salt for 5 minutes in a large microwave safe bowl (rice expands while cooking so choose a suitable bowl that is large enough)
Add the chicken, pepper corns, cinnamon, chopped ginger, butter or ghee and mint
Cover the dish with a lid with holes (or plastic wrap, leaving one side unsealed for venting)
Microwave on high heat for 10 minutes with 5-minute rests each time
Microwave again on high for 5 more minutes
Remove the dish and check if the rice and chicken are cooked, otherwise microwave for 2 more minutes. Do not stir the rice
Fluff with a fork before serving

4. SIMPLE FRIED RICE

Ingredients
2 eggs beaten
¼ cup frozen peas
1 small carrot diced into small pieces
1 cup cooked rice
2 teaspoons soy sauce
2 tablespoons scallions or spring onions
2 tablespoons butter
½ teaspoon crushed pepper

Method
Take a microwave safe dish and add the butter
and beaten eggs. Season with crushed pepper
Microwave on high for 30 minutes
Remove and break up the egg
Mix in the peas, rice, soy sauce with a fork
Microwave for 2 minutes
Fluff with a fork.
Garnish with the scallions / spring onions

5. SIMPLE BEEF PULAO/ PILAF

Ingredients
2 cups Basmati rice or any other long grained
rice
500 grams Beef Tenderloin (with a little fat) cut
into small cubes
½ cup oil or ghee
1 teaspoon chilli powder
2 big onions sliced finely
3 or 4 green chilies sliced lengthwise
2 tablespoons ginger garlic paste

2 big tomatoes chopped
2 tablespoons chopped fresh mint leaves
½ cup coriander leaves (chopped)
1 cup curds (yogurt)
½ teaspoon turmeric powder
2 bay leaves
4 cloves, 3 small sticks of cinnamon, 4 cardamoms
Salt to taste

Method
Marinate the Beef pieces with all the above ingredients overnight in the fridge (except the rice)

Transfer to a large microwave safe dish
Cover the dish with a lid with holes (or plastic wrap, leaving one side unsealed for venting)
Microwave on high for 8 minutes.
Remove and mix well

Microwave again for 6 minutes more till the beef is tender with 3-minute rests

Add the rice and 3 cups of water and mix well
Microwave on high heat for 10 minutes with 5-minute rests each time

Remove the dish and check if the rice and beef are cooked and all the liquid is absorbed, otherwise microwave for 3 more minutes.

Do not stir the rice
Let the Palau stand for about 10 minutes before serving with curd chutney or any curry.

6. MUTTON / LAMB PULAO

Ingredients
2 cups Basmati Rice or any other Good Rice ...
wash and soak for about 1 hour before cooking
300 grams Mutton / Lamb cut into small pieces
2 bay leaves
1 teaspoon all spice powder or garam masala
2 large tomatoes chopped
2 small sticks of cinnamon, 3 cloves, 3 cardamoms
½ cup oil or ghee
Salt to taste
3 green chilies slit lengthwise
2 tablespoons ginger garlic paste
1 teaspoon chillie powder
2 large onions sliced finely
½ teaspoon turmeric powder
½ cup chopped fresh mint leaves
3 tablespoons curds / yogurt

Method
Marinate the mutton or lamb pieces with all the above ingredients overnight in the fridge (except the rice)

Transfer to a large microwave safe dish

Cover the dish with a lid with holes (or plastic wrap, leaving one side unsealed for venting)

Microwave on high for 8 minutes.
Remove and mix well

Microwave again for 6 minutes more till the meat is tender with 3-minute rests

Add the rice and 3 cups of water and mix well

Microwave on high heat for 10 minutes with 5-minute rests each time

Remove the dish and check if the rice and meat are cooked and all the liquid is absorbed, otherwise microwave for 3 more minutes.

Do not stir the rice

Let the Palau stand for about 10 minutes before serving with curd chutney or any curry.

7. CHICKEN PULAO / PILAF

Ingredients
2 cups Basmati rice or any other long grained rice
½ Kg boneless chicken chopped into medium size pieces
½ cup oil or ghee
1 teaspoons chillie powder
2 big onions sliced finely
3 or 4 green chilies sliced lengthwise
2 tablespoons ginger garlic paste
2 big tomatoes chopped
1 pack coconut milk
½ cup chopped coriander leaves
1 cup curds (yogurt)
½ teaspoon turmeric powder
2 bay leaves
4 cloves, 3 small sticks of cinnamon,
4 cardamoms
Salt to taste

Method

Marinate the chicken pieces with all the above ingredients overnight in the fridge (except the rice)

Transfer to a large microwave safe dish when ready to cook

Cover the dish with a lid with holes (or plastic wrap, leaving one side unsealed for venting)

Microwave on high for 8 minutes. Remove and mix well

Microwave again for 6 minutes more till the chicken is tender (with 3-minute rests)

Wash the rice and drain it

Add the rice and 2 cups of water and mix well

Microwave on high heat for 10 minutes (with 5-minute rests each time)

Remove the dish and check if the rice and chicken are cooked and all the liquid is absorbed, otherwise microwave for 2 more minutes.

Do not stir the rice

Let the Palau stand for about 10 minutes before serving with curd chutney or any curry.

8. EGG PULAO / PILAF

Ingredients
½ kg Basmati rice or any other long grained rice
6 hardboiled eggs
2 big onions sliced finely
2 green chilies sliced lengthwise
1 tablespoon ginger garlic paste
2 tablespoons tomato puree or paste
3 tablespoons chopped coriander leaves
2 bay leaves
4 cloves, 4 pieces of cinnamon, 4 cardamoms
1 teaspoon chillie powder
½ teaspoon turmeric powder
½ teaspoon garam masala powder
Salt to taste
2 tablespoons oil
2 tablespoons ghee

Method

Wash and drain the rice

Take a large microwave safe dish and add the oil and ghee

Add the sliced onions, green chillies, bay leaves, cinnamon, cloves and cardamoms

Microwave on high for 2 minutes.

Remove and add the rice and all the other ingredients (except the eggs)

Add 3 cups of water and mix well

Cover the dish with a lid with holes (or plastic wrap, leaving one side unsealed for venting)

Microwave on high heat for 10 minutes (with 5-minute rests each time)

Remove the dish and add the boiled eggs and mix in lightly

Microwave for 3 more minutes
Do not stir the rice

Let the Pulao stand for about 10 minutes before serving with curd chutney or any curry.

9. PEAS PULAO

Ingredients
2 cups basmati rice or any other raw rice
2 onions sliced finely,
1 teaspoon ginger garlic paste
¼ cup oil or ghee
Salt to taste
3 green chilies chopped
1 teaspoon chillie powder
2 Bay leaves
4 cloves, 2 pieces cinnamon, 3 cardamoms

Method
Wash and drain the rice
Take a large microwave safe dish and add the oil and ghee
Add the sliced onions, green chillies, bay leaves, cinnamon, cloves and cardamoms

Microwave on high for 1.5 minutes.

Remove and add the rice, peas and all the other ingredients. Add 3 cups of water and mix well

Cover the dish with a lid with holes (or plastic wrap, leaving one side unsealed for venting)

Microwave on high heat for 10 minutes (with 5-minute rests each time)

Remove and check if the rice is cooked, otherwise microwave for 2 or 3 minutes more

Do not stir the rice

Let the Pulao stand for about 10 minutes before serving with curd chutney or any curry.

10. MICROWAVE MIXED VEGETABLE PULAO

Ingredients
1 Cup Basmati Rice
3 tablespoons Ghee
2 tablespoons Oil
1 small piece of Cinnamon
1 teaspoon Ginger Garlic Paste
3 green Chilies
4 Cloves
1 piece of cinnamon
3 cardamoms
1 bay leaf
1 Small Onion sliced
1 Carrot diced into small pieces
½ cup Green Peas
Salt to taste

Method

Wash and drain the rice

Take a large microwave safe dish and add the oil and ghee

Add the sliced onions, green chillies, bay leaf, cinnamon, cloves and cardamoms

Microwave on high for 2 minutes.

Remove and add the rice, peas, carrots and all the other ingredients

Add 2 cups of water and mix well

Cover the dish with a lid with holes (or plastic wrap, leaving one side unsealed for venting)

Microwave on high heat for 10 minutes (with 5-minute rests each time)

Remove and check if the rice is cooked, otherwise microwave for 2 or 3 minutes more

Do not stir the rice

Let the Pulao stand for about 10 minutes before serving.

Serve with curd chutney or raita or any curry.

15. MICROWAVE DESSERTS AND CAKES

1. BREAD PUDDING IN A CUP

Ingredients
1 or 2 slices of bread, cubed
1 tablespoon butter
1 egg
3 tablespoons milk
1/4 teaspoon cinnamon
1/2 teaspoon vanilla extract (optional)

Method
Melt butter in a microwave safe cup or mug for 10 seconds in the microwave.
Remove and swirl it around the mug
Add the bread to the mug.
In a separate cup, combine the egg, milk, cinnamon, and vanilla. Stir well.
Pour this liquid over the bread. Swirl it a little and allow the liquid to soak into the bread.
Place the mug in the Microwave.
Microwave on high for one minute, then add ten seconds at a time until it's cooked to your liking (no runny eggs).
It takes around 1 minute 30 seconds.
Add syrup if desired.

2. APPLE PIE

Ingredients
6 Marie biscuits or Digestive Biscuits
1 tablespoon butter
1 green apple, cored, peeled, and cut into small chunks.
1 tablespoon plain flour
1 tablespoon powdered sugar
1/2 teaspoon cinnamon powder
1 teaspoon lemon or lime juice

Method
Place cookies in a plastic bag and smash into crumbs.
Place the butter in a microwave safe bowl and melt in the microwave for 10 seconds
Add the biscuit crumbs to the bowl and mash with fingers to coat the crumbs with the melted butter.

Press down well. Keep a little of the crumbs aside for the top of the pie.

In another bowl mix the apple chunks, flour, powdered sugar, cinnamon powder and lime juice together

Place this bowl in the microwave.

Microwave on high for 2 minutes to soften the apple. This is the apple pie filling

Now transfer the apple pie filling into bowl with the biscuit crust

Top up the pie with the leftover biscuit crumbs for a little crunch and microwave for 30 seconds.

Serve with some whipped cream.

3. OATS AND BLUEBERRY COBBLER

Ingredients

½ cup instant oats, uncooked

1 egg

½ cup milk (add a little more milk if too thick)

½ teaspoon cinnamon

2 teaspoons honey

1/3 cup fresh or frozen blueberries

2 teaspoons butter

Method

Mix all the ingredients (except the blueberries) together

Once it's all mixed well, gently mix in the blueberries

Transfer to a microwave safe bowl or dish

Place the bowl in the microwave and microwave on high for 2 minutes

Remove and mix gently.

Microwave on high again for one more minute.

Eat with cream if desired

4. CHOCOLATE CHIP COOKIE IN A MUG

Ingredients
3 tablespoons All-Purpose Flour
1 tablespoon Brown Sugar
¼ teaspoon salt
¼ teaspoon vanilla essence
¼ teaspoon baking powder
1 tablespoon melted butter
1 egg beaten (optional)
2 tablespoons chocolate chips or chunks

Method

Combine all the ingredients together in a microwave safe mug

Place in the microwave and microwave on high for 90 seconds.

Enjoy it with Ice Cream

5. CINNAMON MUFFIN IN A MUG

Ingredients
4 tablespoons Flour
¼ teaspoon baking powder
3 tablespoons milk
1 tablespoon vegetable oil or butter
1 tablespoon sugar
¼ teaspoon vanilla essence or extract
1/4 teaspoon salt
1 teaspoon cinnamon powder

Method
Combine all the ingredients together and transfer to a microwave safe ramekin or cup

Place in the microwave and microwave on high for 90 minutes

Serve with a cup of coffee

6. STRAWBERRY CHEESE CAKE

Ingredients
6 tablespoons crushed Digestive Biscuits or any Biscuits of your choice
1 tablespoon melted Butter
10 tablespoons Cream Cheese
2 Egg Whites beaten
5 tablespoon Sugar
2 teaspoons All-Purpose Flour
½ teaspoon Vanilla Essence or Extract
2 tablespoons Strawberry Jam

Method

Crush the Biscuits well and mix with the melted butter

Press the mixture down on the bottom of a microwave glass dish

In a separate bowl, combine the Cream Cheese, Egg Whites, Sugar, Flour and Vanilla Essence together. Beat till well combined and creamy

Pour on the crushed biscuit base in the dish

Place in the Microwave and microwave on high for 2 minutes

Spread the strawberry Jam on top immediately so that the jam melts and seeps through.
Serve as individual slices

7. CHOCOLATE CAKE

Ingredients
½ cup Flour
5 tablespoons Sugar
4 tablespoons Cocoa Powder
½ teaspoon Baking Powder
¼ teaspoon Salt
3 tablespoons Vegetable Oil
6 tablespoons Milk
½ teaspoon Vanilla Essence or Extract

Method

Combine all the ingredients together

Transfer to a greased Microwave safe dish

Microwave on high for 90 seconds. Check if cooked or microwave again for 1 minute

Top with melted Chocolate if desired

Transfer to a plate when cold. Cut into slices and enjoy with ice cream or chocolate sauce

8. APPLE CAKE

Ingredients
1 apple peeled and chopped into small chunks
½ cup flour
½ cup of breakfast oats
½ teaspoon cinnamon
¼ teaspoon salt
4 tablespoons cooking oil
3 tablespoons brown sugar
Method

Mix all the ingredients together (except the apple) until the batter is smooth
Mix in the chopped apple gently
Transfer to a greased microwave dish
Sprinkle some sliced almonds on top if desired
Place in the microwave and microwave on high for 90 seconds
Set aside to cool then turn cut into wedges

9. CHOCOLATE LAVA MUG CAKE

Ingredients
3 tablespoons flour
1 tablespoon cocoa powder
¼ teaspoon baking powder
2 tablespoons milk
1 tablespoon cooking oil
¼ teaspoon vanilla essence
1 tablespoon brown sugar

Method
Mix all the ingredients together in a big
Microwave safe Mug or cup

Microwave on high for 2 minutes

Enjoy your chocolate lava cake cold or warm

10. BANANA WALNUT CAKE

Ingredients

1 ripe banana
2 tablespoons cooking oil
1 egg beaten
½ cup flour
1 teaspoon baking powder
3 tablespoons brown sugar
½ teaspoon vanilla essence or extract
3 tablespoons milk

Method
Mash the banana well

Mix the mashed banana with all the other
ingredients

Transfer to a greased microwave safe dish

Microwave on high for 3 minutes

Check if cooked inside by inserting a toothpick,
otherwise microwave for 2 more minutes

16. MICROWAVE FESTIVE SWEETS AND TREATS

1. ALMOND AND WHITE CHOCOLATE FUDGE

Ingredients

1 can Sweetened condensed milk (not evaporated milk)
500 grams good quality white chocolate chips (3 cups approximately)
1 teaspoon vanilla essence
¼ cup chopped roasted almonds or any other nuts of your choice

Method
Line a 7 or 8 " square pan with parchment paper
or wax paper. Double line it for easy removal of
the fudge.

Heat up condensed milk in a microwave safe
bowl for 1 minute on high heat. This will loosen
it up a bit.

Now stir in the white chocolate to the same bowl.
Microwave white chocolate chips and the
sweetened condensed milk together on high for 1
minute, stirring every 30 seconds until chocolate
is completely melted.

Take it out of the microwave. Let it stand for 5
seconds and gently stir.

Repeat the process of microwaving in 30 seconds
each time until the chocolate melts completely
and the mixture is smooth.
(Give it a light stir after each 30 seconds)

It takes around 3 minutes in total to melt the
chocolate chips.

Once melted add in the vanilla essence and
roasted almonds or nuts

Transfer the mixture to the lined pan and level it
with a spatula or back of a spoon.

Leave aside to cool or place in the fridge

After it is set, take it out of the pan and cut into
squares with a sharp knife

2. SIMPLE CHOCOLATE FUDGE

Ingredients
3 cups chocolate chips
1 can condensed milk
4 tablespoons unsalted butter
1 teaspoon vanilla essence or extract
¼ teaspoon salt

Method
Line an 8x8 inch pan with aluminum foil and grease it

Combine the chocolate chips, condensed milk, and butter in a large microwave safe bowl

Microwave on high for one minute and stir.
Repeat the process of microwaving in 30 seconds each time until the chocolate melts completely and the mixture is smooth.
(Give it a light stir after each 30 seconds)

It takes around 3 minutes in total to melt the chocolate chips and become like fudge

Microwave for 1 more minute if you desire it to be firm

Transfer the mixture to the lined pan and level it with a spatula or back of a spoon.

Leave aside to cool or place in the fridge

After it is set, take it out of the pan and cut into squares with a sharp knife

3. VANILLA FUDGE

Ingredients
100 grams butter
1 cup sugar
1 can condensed milk
4 tablespoons golden syrup or butterscotch syrup
1 teaspoon vanilla essence or extract

Method
Line an 8x8 inch pan with aluminium foil and grease it

Combine all the ingredients together in a large microwave safe bowl

Microwave on high for one minute then remove and stir

Microwave on high again for 2 minutes. Remove and stir
Repeat the process of microwaving in 2 minutes each time for a total of 12 minutes till the mixture is smooth and becomes like fudge

Microwave for 1 more minute if you desire it to be firm

Transfer the mixture to the lined pan and level it with a spatula or back of a spoon.
Leave aside to cool or place in the fridge
After it is set, take it out of the pan and cut into squares with a sharp knife

4. WALNUT AND RAISIN FUDGE

Ingredients
3 cups chocolate chips
1 can condensed milk
1 cup sugar
½ cup raisins
½ cup roasted walnut pieces
1 teaspoon vanilla essence

Method
Line an 8x8 inch pan with aluminum foil and grease it

Combine all the ingredients (except the raisins, walnuts and vanilla) together in a large microwave safe glass bowl

Microwave on high for one minute then remove and stir

Microwave on high again for 2 minutes. Remove and stir

Repeat the process of microwaving in 2 minutes each time for a total of 12 minutes till the mixture is smooth and becomes like fudge

Quickly stir in the raisins, walnuts and vanilla.

Pour the mixture into the prepared pan and refrigerate until set

Cut into pieces when set

5. COCONUT SWEET / BARFI / CANDY

Ingredients
2 cups desiccated coconut flakes
1.5 cups sugar
4 tablespoons soogi (optional)
2 tablespoons ghee or butter
1 teaspoon vanilla essence
A pinch of salt
¾ cup water

Method
Grease a suitable plate and keep ready

Mix the sugar and water together in a microwave safe bowl
Microwave on high for 4 minutes. Remove the dish and stir
Microwave for 3 minutes. Remove and Stir
Microwave again for 3 minutes and stir.
The syrup will be of one string consistency
Add the coconut flakes, soogi, ghee / butter, vanilla essence & salt to the syrup and mix well.

Microwave for 2 minutes. Remove and stir
Microwave it for another 3 minutes
Check if the mixture is watery otherwise microwave for 2 or 3 minutes more

Pour the coconut mixture on the greased plate and spread it evenly

Allow it to cool & cut it into desired shape when still warm

6. ALMOND SWEET

Ingredients

1cup Almond Flour
2 tablespoons ghee or butter
¼ cup warm water
½ cup Sugar
1teaspoon almond essence

Method

Mix the sugar and water together in a microwave safe bowl till the sugar is dissolved

Add the almond flour, ghee and essence and mix well together

Microwave for 2 minutes.

Remove and Stir

Microwave again for 2 minutes and stir.

At this stage the mixture would thicken and come together as a soft, pliable ball.

Transfer to a greased plate.

Press down well

Cut into diamond shapes when cool

Note: You could add a drop of any food colouring of your choice if you desire

7. DHOL DHOL / DODOL
(BLACK RICE HALWA)

Ingredients
1 cup Black Puttu Rice Flour or Black Glutinous
Rice Flour
1.5 cups sugar
400 ml coconut milk or coconut cream
A pinch of salt
3 tablespoons ghee
1 teaspoon vanilla essence
1 teaspoon almond essence
½ cup almond slivers or cashew nut (optional)

Method
Grease a suitable plate and keep ready

In a microwave safe bowl mix together the black
puttu rice flour, sugar, coconut milk, salt and
ghee.
Microwave on high for 3 minutes. Remove and
stir
Microwave on high for 3 minutes. Remove the
dish and stir
Microwave for 2 more minutes. Remove and Stir

Add 1 tablespoon more of ghee, almond essence
and slivered almonds or cashews.
Mix well and microwave on high for 3 minutes.
Take out, stir and microwave on high for 2
minutes more. Stir again

The mixture should be of halwa consistency.
Pour on to the greased plate and leave to cool
Cut into diamonds when cold

8. SIMPLE RICE AND MILK PUDDING

Ingredients
½ cup Basmati Rice or any raw rice of your choice
2 cups water
1 cup milk
¼ cup sugar
1 teaspoon vanilla essence
A few roasted nuts to garnish

Method

Wash the rice and soak in 2 cups of water and a pinch of salt for 5 minutes in a large microwave safe bowl (rice expands while cooking so choose a suitable bowl that is large enough)

Microwave on high heat for 10 minutes with 5-minute rests
At this point, small steam holes will appear in the rice and most of the water would be absorbed
Add the milk, vanilla essence and sugar and stir well
Now cover the dish with a lid with holes (or plastic wrap, leaving one side unsealed for venting)
Microwave on high for 8 minutes more, with 2-minute rests in between.
Remove and stir each time. This helps dissolve the sugar better and makes sure the milk doesn't spill over.
Garnish with roasted nuts and serve.

9. VERMCELLI PUDDING

Ingredients
½ cup Vermicelli
½ cup sugar
½ cup warm water
2 cups milk
1 tablespoon ghee
1 teaspoon vanilla essence
¼ cup roasted cashew nuts

Method

Mix the vermicelli with the ghee and microwave on high for 30 seconds

Remove and mix it then microwave again for 30 seconds more

Add the water and 1 cup of milk and mix well

Now cover the dish with a lid with holes (or plastic wrap, leaving one side unsealed for venting)

Microwave on high for 3 minutes

Remove and mix well. Microwave again on high for 2 minutes

Remove and mix in the sugar, remaining milk and vanilla essence. Mix well

Microwave on high for 3 minutes, stirring in between twice after 1 min.

Remove and mix in the roasted cashews

Microwave for 1 more minute then remove

Serve hot or cold.

Add a little warm milk before serving if required

10. SEMOLINA PUDDING

Ingredients

½ cup Semolina (Soogi /Rawa)
1.5 cups milk
¼ cup sugar (Add more if desired)
2 tablespoons ghee
1teaspoon vanilla essence
1 cup of water

Method

Mix the semolina with the ghee and microwave on high for 30 seconds

Remove and mix it well, then microwave again for 30 seconds more

Add the water and 1 cup of milk and mix well

Now cover the dish with a lid with holes (or plastic wrap, leaving one side unsealed for venting)

Microwave on high for 3 minutes
Remove and mix well.
Microwave again on high for 2 minutes

Remove and mix in the sugar and vanilla essence or cardamom powder.

Mix well

Microwave on high for 3 minutes, with 1-minute rests stirring in between twice after 1 min.

Serve hot.

17. SOME BASIC CURRY POWDERS THAT COULD BE MADE AT HOME

In this section, a few basic preparations such as curry powders that could be used for every day cooking are featured. These powders can be stored for 6 to 8 months and are better than the readymade masala powders available in the shops.

1. BASIC CHILLIE POWDER

Ingredients
½ kg Red Chilies (long or round variety for pungency)
½ kg Kashmiri Chilies or any other variety (for adding colour)

Roast the two types of chilies in a microwave safe dish for 2 minutes on High. You may need to do them in batches.

The chillies should turn quite crisp. Leave aside to cool
Powder them at home in the dry blender or get it done at the mill.

Note: This chillie powder can be used for any type of dish that calls for chillie powder. It can be stored for more than a year

2. ANGLO-INDIAN CURRY POWDER

Ingredients
¼ kg Red Chilies for pungency
½ kg Kashmiri Chilies or any other non-spicy variety for colour
500 grams coriander seeds
200 grams cumin seeds
100 grams pepper corns
100 grams mustard seeds

Method
Roast the above ingredients separately in a microwave safe dish for 2 minutes each on High. You may need to do them in batches. The chillies should turn quite crisp
Leave aside to cool
Powder them at home in the dry blender or get it done at the mill.

Note: A teaspoon or two of this powder can be used for almost all curries both vegetarian and non- vegetarian. It can be stored and used for more than a year.

3. ANGLO-INDIAN PEPPERWATER POWDER

Ingredients
¼ kg Red Chilies
100 grams pepper corns
100 grams cumin seeds
20 grams turmeric powder

Method

Roast the above ingredients separately in a microwave safe dish for 2 minutes each on High. Leave aside to cool
Powder them at home in the dry blender or get it done at the mill.

Note: 2 teaspoons of this powder should be added to 2 cups of water, 2 tomatoes chopped, a lump of tamarind and a little salt and cooked for 5 minutes to make instant pepper water.

The pepper water should be tempered with mustard, garlic and curry leaves

4. ANGLO-INDIAN VINDALOO POWDER

Ingredients
½ kg red chillies
¼ kg kashmiri chillies or any other variety for colour
100 grams cumin seeds
100 grams mustard seeds
100 grams pepper corns
2 tablespoons turmeric powder

Roast the above ingredients separately in a microwave safe dish for 2 minutes each on High. You may need to do them in batches. The chillies should turn quite crisp
Leave aside to cool
Powder them at home in the dry blender or get it done at the mill.

Note: 2 teaspoons of this powder could be used while preparing Vindaloo using ½ kg of meat

5. ANGLO-INDIAN SPICE POWDER (GARAM MASALA POWDER)

Ingredients
2 teaspoons pepper corns
10 to 12 cloves
8 cardamoms
6 small sticks of cinnamon
1 Bay leaf
1 tablespoon fennel or saunf

Method
Roast the above ingredients separately in a microwave safe dish for 2 minutes each on High
Leave aside to cool
Powder them at home in the dry blender or get it done at the mill.

Note: This spice powder can be used for any recipe that calls for all spice powder.

ABOUT THE AUTHOR
BRIDGET WHITE-KUMAR

Bridget White-Kumar was born and brought up in Kolar Gold Fields, a small mining town in the erstwhile Mysore State (now known as Karnataka), in India, which was famous for its Colonial ambiance. She comes from a well-known Anglo-Indian family who lived and worked in KGF for many generations.

Bridget is a Cookery Book Author, Food Consultant and Culinary Historian. She has authored 7 Recipe books on Anglo-Indian Cuisine.

Her area of expertise is in Colonial Anglo-Indian Food and she has gone through a lot of effort in reviving the old forgotten dishes of the Colonial British Raj Era. Her 7 Recipe books are a means of preserving for posterity, the very authentic tastes and flavours of Colonial 'Anglo- Indian Food' besides recording for future generations, the unique heritage of the pioneers of Anglo-Indian Cuisine.

Her Recipe Book ANGLO-INDIAN CUISINE – A LEGACY OF FLAVOURS FROM THE PAST was selected as 'Winner from India' under the Category: 'BEST CULINARY HISTORY BOOK'. by GOURMAND INTERNATIONAL SPAIN, WORLD COOK BOOK AWARDS 2012

Bridget is also an Independent Freelance Consultant on Food Related matters. She has assisted many Restaurants, Hotels and Clubs in Bangalore and elsewhere in India with her knowledge of Colonial Anglo-Indian Food besides helping them to revamp and reinvent their Menus by introducing new dishes which are a combination of both Continental and Anglo-Indian. Many of them are now following the Recipes and guidance given by her and the dishes are enjoyed by both Indian and Foreign Guests.

Bridget also conducts Cooking Demonstrations and Workshops at various places across the country such as Clubs, Restaurants, Women's Groups, Corporate Offices, etc. She is always ready to share and talk about Recipes and Food. She can be contacted on +919845571254

Email:
bridgetkumar@yahoo.com
bidkumar@gmail.com

Websites:
http://bridget-white.com
http://anglo-indianfood.blogspot.com
http://anglo-indianrecipes.blogspot.com

19. ANGLO-INDIAN COOKERY BOOKS BY BRIDGET WHITE

1.ANGLO-INDIAN CUISINE – A LEGACY OF FLAVOURS FROM THE PAST is a comprehensive and unique collection of easy- to- follow Recipes of popular and well-loved Anglo-Indian dishes. The repertoire is rich and vast, ranging from the outright European Cutlets, Croquettes, pasties, roasts, etc., to mouth- watering Curries, Side dishes, Spicy Fries, Foogaths, Biryani and Palau, Pickles, Chutneys etc., picking up plenty of hybrids along the way.

This book was selected as the Winner from India at the Gourmand Cook Book Award 2012 under the category 'BEST CULINARY HISTORY BOOK FROM INDIA'

2. A COLLECTION OF SIMPLE ANGLO-INDIAN RECIPES is a revised, consolidated version of four earlier Recipe Books of Bridget White, namely Bridget's Anglo-Indian Delicacies, A Collection of Anglo-Indian Roasts, Casseroles and Bakes, The Anglo-Indian Snack Box &The Anglo-Indian Festive Hamper.

More than 350 Recipes of traditional, popular and well loved, Anglo-Indian Dishes have been specially selected from these earlier Cook Books and featured in this Omni-bus Edition. The huge selection of Anglo-Indian dishes featured in this Cookery book will surely take one on a sentimental and nostalgic journey down memory lane of old forgotten Anglo-Indian Culinary Delights.

3. ANGLO-INDIAN DELICACIES is a collection of Recipes of popular vintage and contemporary Cuisine of Colonial India such as Pork Bhooni, Devil Pork Curry, Calcutta Cutlets, Fish Kedegeree, Double Onions Meat Curry, Camp Soup, Bengal Lancers Shrimp Curry, etc. This Cookery Book would also serve as a 'Ready Reckoner' and a useful guide for teaming up dishes for everyday Anglo-Indian Meals as well as for festive and special occasions.

4.THE ANGLO-INDIAN FESTIVE HAMPER is a collection of popular Anglo-Indian Festive and Holiday Treats, such as Cakes, Sweets, Christmas goodies, Puddings, Sandwiches, Preserves, Home-made Wines, etc.

5. THE ANGLO-INDIAN SNACK BOX is a collection of simple and easy to follow recipes of tasty Vegetarian and Non-Vegetarian snacks, short eats, nibbles and finger food, which includes savouries, sandwiches, wraps, rolls, pastries, sweets etc.

6. A COLLECTION OF ANGLO-INDIAN ROASTS, CASSEROLES AND BAKES is a practical and easy guide to the preparation of a variety of Anglo-Indian Roasts, Casseroles and Bakes such as Shepherd's Pie, Washerman's Pie, Roast Chicken, Roast Turkey, etc.

7. ANGLO-INDIAN TEA TIME TREATS - A touch of Nostalgia is a selection of easy-to-make popular Afternoon Tea Recipes. The selection includes, traditional British Tea time treats such as Doughnuts, Scones, Tea time cakes, besides a huge variety of traditional and contemporary sandwiches. A wide selection of savoury Anglo- Indian tea time snacks and small bites are also featured in this collection. This collection of recipes of old traditional delights will surely bring on the nostalgia!

20. OTHER COOKERY BOOKS BY BRIDGET WHITE

1. VEGETARIAN DELICACIES is a collection of simple and easy recipes of delectable Vegetarian Dishes. The repertoire is rich and vast, ranging from simple Soups and Salads, to mouth-watering Curries, Stir fries, Rice dishes, Casseroles and Baked Dishes and popular Accompaniments.

2. SIMPLE EGG DELICACIES is a collection of simple and easy recipes of delectable Egg Dishes for Breakfast, Lunch and Dinner and for all other times as well. The repertoire ranges from simple Breakfast Egg Dishes and Egg Salads, to mouth-watering Curries, Tea Time treats, Sandwiches, Casseroles and Baked Dishes. A real treat for 'Eggetarians'.

3. COOKING WITHOUT FIRE – No Flame, No Fire Recipes" is a delightful collection of easy to make dishes that require no cooking or heating. The repertoire ranges from Simple Salads, Scrumptious Sandwiches, Wraps and Rolls with a Twist, Small Bites, Savoury Quickies & Finger Foods, Delectable Delights, Desserts and Sweet Treats, Smoothies and Shakes. The Recipes call for ingredients that are easily available at home and are quick and easy to prepare, besides being tasty, healthy and nutritious. The options for using the recipes to make and enjoy these delicious treats in this book are endless.

4. DELECTABLE KEBABS AND SIMPLE PILAFS is a collection of simple and easy recipes of popular Indian Kebabs and Pilafs. It is a useful handbook for anyone who wants to prepare simple and tasty Kebabs and Pilafs. It tells you exactly what ingredients are needed and guides you step by step through the process with the least amount of effort. Only easily available ingredients have been made use of. These kebabs could be prepared at an outdoor BBQ or grilled in the oven in your kitchen.

Printed in Great Britain
by Amazon